The
Tales
Behind
TAROT

DISCOVER THE STORIES
WITHIN YOUR TAROT CARDS

**ALISON
DAVIES**

**Foreword by
The Witch of the Forest**

Leaping Hare Press

The Suit of Wands

The Suit of Cups

FOREWORD

I've been a Witch and tarot practitioner now for 16 years. As well as reading the cards for myself, my family and friends, I have also been reading tarot professionally for others for about 5 years now and I can truly say that I wish this book had been available when I started my own journey with tarot! I remember how overwhelmed I felt when I was trying to learn about the different meanings and energies of all 78 cards. This is a very common and completely natural feeling, but with Alisons incredible gift for storytelling, this book shows us there is another way: one that makes starting your own tarot journey much less daunting and stressful.

By telling the short story of each card at a time, the book is set out in a way that makes tarot accessible to everyone, regardless of any prior knowledge or practice. This makes it the perfect book for those at the beginning of their own tarot journey as it provides the perfect place to start, but because of the detail included in the story for each card, this book can undoubtably help enrich and develop the practice of more experienced readers and expand their knowledge. Even after 16 years of practice, Alison has helped to deepen my understanding of the cards; words are her magick as she weaves the fundamental meaning of each card with each story she tells.

At the heart of this book, it shows that the meanings of the cards in a tarot deck do not stand separate from each other. They are far better understood when they are put together, which is what this book achieves beautifully. When the cards are together, a story unfolds that helps the reader connect with the core meanings of each card, and to remember them and absorb the information.

In the 22 cards of the Major Arcana, we follow The Fool's Journey. In the 56 cards from the Minor Arcana, we follow a different journey for Swords, Wands, Cups, and Pentacles which really helps to form a deeper understanding of what each card means, as well as its place within the suit from which it came. Alison helps us to see that each card is a small piece of a larger puzzle, that when placed together, offers greater insight into many areas of life.

I highly recommend *Tales Behind Tarot* to budding readers and experienced practitioners alike. So make your favorite hot drink, find somewhere comfy and immerse yourself in the stories.

Much love,

Lindsay x

(*The Witch of the Forest*)

INTRODUCTION

Beautiful, beguiling, and infused with mystery, the Tarot may resemble an ordinary pack of playing cards, but it is so much more. Yes, there are obvious similarities, like the four suits of cups, pentacles, wands, and swords, which relate to the hearts, diamonds, clubs, and spades in the playing cards, but it is the distinct differences that make these colorful decks so captivating.

Unlike playing cards, the Tarot is formed of two sections called Arcanas. The Major Arcana contains an array of standalone picture cards, while the Minor Arcana houses all the suits. Together, these two parts make a whole pack containing seventy-eight cards, which can be used in a number of ways. Traditionally the Tarot was thought of as a fortune-telling tool. Cards would be selected at random and laid out in different spreads to predict the future (divination). While this might sound simple, there are many facets to a Tarot reading, not just divining what destiny has in store. Over the years readings have developed to encompass other aspects, like insights into the past and present, spiritual advice and even suggestions for taking action. The cards are commonly used as a problem-solving tool, but in their simplest form they can provide inspiration and something to reflect upon. It's no wonder the Tarot speaks to us at a deep soul level. Whether you're a lifelong enthusiast or quietly intrigued, you can't deny the charm of these cards. With powerful images that resonate with the psyche, and equally potent themes that are easily distinguishable, mystics and skeptics agree on their allure.

At first glance you'll notice the intricate pictures. In most decks these are colorful and vibrant to catch the eye, making them a joy to behold and also inspiring should you wish to use them creatively. Look a little closer and you'll connect with the heart of the card. You'll see that each carefully crafted image is littered with signs and symbols that, if deciphered, will help you understand its true nature.

Put the cards together in order and you'll see a story unfold, a narrative that not only helps you connect with the meanings but is also something you can identify with. This is because the Tarot deals with issues and experiences we have all witnessed or encountered, so rather than being some otherworldly tool or occult mystery as they are often considered, the reality is they're accessible to everyone. As such the cards are a gift that can brighten and enlighten your world, but where did the idea originally come from?

THE ORIGINS OF THE TAROT

Most scholars agree that the Tarot was invented in Italy in the 1430s as a popular parlor game. Like normal playing cards, each pack held four suits, but there was an additional fifth suit of twenty-one trumps, known as *"Trionfi,"* with an extra card called *"il matto,"* meaning "The Fool." The trumps were decorated with colorful images of people, animals, and re-enactments of Roman processions, and were considered more powerful than any of the four suits. The first known Tarot deck was commissioned by the Duke of Milan, Filippo Visconti, and his son-in-law Francesco Sforza in 1425. Named the Visconti-Sforza deck, these beautiful cards were individually hand-painted. Over time the Tarot spread through Europe, reaching the farthest corners of the Earth, growing in popularity and spiritual significance.

The most influential deck in the world, and the one upon which many modern Tarot packs are modeled, was created by two members of the Golden Dawn; the mystic and spiritual seeker A. E. Waite, and the clairvoyant artist and illustrator Pamela Colman Smith. Together they fashioned images that drew upon Egyptian and Christian symbolism, along with astrological attributions to craft the deck that is featured in this book. At the time Smith's name was replaced by the publishers but has since been reinstated and the cards are now known as the Rider-Waite-Smith deck.

HOW TO USE THIS BOOK

Whether you are a regular Tarot reader or new to the practice, you'll discover that sometimes the cards will fall just so, to reveal uncanny insights about you and your life, at any given moment. Like picking up your favorite book and letting the pages fall open, the Tarot reveals a chapter at a time, and the potential outcomes depending on the choices you make. It is a blueprint designed to help you make the most of every day.

This book is a guide that will help you connect with the images and interpret the hidden themes, based on the Rider-Waite-Smith deck. By reading the tales behind the Tarot, you'll not only understand the meaning, but also where the card sits in the bigger picture, whether that's within its specific suit, or the Fool's Journey of the Major Arcana. You'll be able to apply the narrative to your own life and use it to navigate the twists and turns of fate. Stories have long been used as tools to help us make sense of the world, allowing us to experience things objectively and develop different perspectives. They also help us retain information, because they sit in the memory and are easy to recall, so the tales behind the Tarot will also help you remember the meaning of each card when you're doing a reading.

How you use this book is up to you. Some readers are naturally drawn to the Major Arcana, and prefer to get to know these cards first, since they are the trumps of the pack. Others might be called to a specific suit that resonates with them. Where you start in the book is not as important as where you start in the narrative. Working your way logically through each longer tale from beginning to end will help you get an overall feeling for each suit, and for the Major and Minor Arcana. Knowing where that card sits in the story will give you a greater understanding of its meaning and you'll also be able to interpret surrounding cards in a reading, by making narrative connections between them. You can then go back and dip into specific cards when you want to refresh your memory or connect at a deeper level. You can also incorporate the tales into your reading, taking extracts to help you make sense of the overall message.

The stories are not set in stone, and every Tarot reader will have their own ideas of how the tale might unfold, but while the narratives might differ in character and plot, the tone and concept are the same. Once you've worked your way through the book, you may want to create your own Tarot tales to help you make sense of the cards, and that's fine. The Tarot is a wonderful tool that can stoke the imagination and help you express yourself in new and creative ways.

The handy references at the back of the book will also help you find out more about the cards, and take your studies even further. The most important thing to remember as you delve into the divinatory world of the Tarot is that it is a personal journey, not unlike that of the Fool in the Major Arcana. Your experience of each card is as unique as you are.

Enjoy, reflect, and revel in the tales behind the Tarot.

THE FOOL.

THE MAGICIAN.

THE HIGH PRIESTESS

THE EMPRESS.

THE EMPEROR.

THE HIEROPHANT

THE LOVERS.

THE CHARIOT.

STRENGTH.

THE HERMIT.

WHEEL of FORTUNE

JUSTICE.

THE HANGEDMAN.

DEATH.

TEMPERANCE.

THE DEVIL.

THE TOWER.

THE STAR.

THE MOON.

THE SUN.

JUDGEMENT.

THE WORLD.

The Major Arcana

Also known as the trumps, the Major Arcana are twenty-two standalone cards that feature in the tarot pack. Unlike the suits, they do not deal with one particular theme throughout, but they do represent a journey and the cycles of life. In this case it's the Fool's journey, the only card without a number. He is the main character in this narrative and each and every card that follows tells his tale.

With a combination of potent images and karmic lessons, these cards strike a powerful chord within our psyche, helping to address deep-seated fears and desires. They also raise the important questions so that we can establish who we are and our life's true purpose. These cards depict the big changes that we face, the things that might turn our life upside down, or give us a second chance. They deal with love, loss, fortune, and the twists and turns of fate, of which there are many.

Some may shy away from the Major Arcana for fear of the unexpected, but they offer the potential to make magic and fulfill your dearest dreams. Should one of these cards crop up in a reading, then pay attention—you're being called to learn an important life lesson and reflect upon the themes therein. It may be that you're already aware of certain issues, or that you need some guidance. The other surrounding cards should help to point you in the right direction. We all face decisions at different times in our life, and the Major Arcana cards are there to help. By reading the Fool's journey, you will form a deeper understanding of what each one means, and the areas that you need to address. You'll realize each card has a positive influence that you can work with to shape your own reality.

THE FOOL.

0 THE FOOL

THEMES

THEMES

New beginnings

Childlike wonder

Innocence

Spontaneity

ONCE UPON A TIME THERE LIVED A FOOL, a young boy with the world at his feet and a dream in his heart. So full of joy was he, that he walked in a daze and lived in the here and now. Some might say his head was full of air, but they would be wrong. The Fool was fully aware of every single thing, for he engaged all of his senses and moved through life with ease. It's true he had much to learn, but he also had much to teach, for when you wander as a fool, you wander freely with openness and this allows you to fully connect with your surroundings.

The Fool was flamboyant. He dressed in bright colors, with artistic flair, and he carried in his hand a white flower as a symbol of his youthful innocence. It wasn't an image; it was simply the way he was. Everything was on show, for the Fool was not accustomed to the ways of the world and had yet to begin his spiritual journey. This excited him greatly. He had been waiting for the right moment, the optimum second when he would take a leap of faith into the unknown. Those who knew him would say he was a dreamer, and those who didn't assumed it was fear that held him back, when in fact it was the opposite. The Fool was brave and bold, a spontaneous soul who was prepared to take a chance.

He packed lightly for his journey, for what was the point of weighing himself down? He had no preconceptions, or expectations. This boy was a book waiting to be filled with adventure. His only companion was a small, white dog, a faithful and loyal friend that had come to wave him off on his travels.

The Fool hadn't planned for this quest, for how can you plan for the future? His blind faith would keep him safe, and he hoped that his encounters would be fortunate. There was no guile in his manner, just an optimism that most who met him found contagious. He had always been a playful boy, the type of character who could find fun anywhere, and because of this he had built a reputation and been given his name—the Fool.

And so it was that on a glorious summer's day when the sun had set the sky alight with its golden rays, the Fool said his goodbyes to all he knew and loved. Today was the day for a new beginning. He could sense it and, driven by the slightest of whims, he decided to take the plunge. With his knapsack over his shoulder, he stepped out into the world. Taking long, purposeful strides, he embraced the air and gulped it down into his lungs. He turned his face upward and delighted at the warmth upon his cheeks. He held the white flower aloft, as if it was an offering to the gods, and he continued to walk one foot in front of the other.

It was almost like a dance for him, a performance, and he enjoyed every second. His steps formed a rhythm that matched the beating of his heart, and soon he had picked up speed and the walk became a trot. Light of foot he sprang forward, as the mountains rose up behind him. To any onlooker this might have seemed a foreboding omen, but not to the Fool. He was oblivious, so caught up in the excitement of the moment that nothing else mattered. His little dog galloped at his side, yapping with glee; he was the only one that could match his companion's enthusiasm. Together they were lost in the dance, which is why the Fool never noticed the edge of the cliff as it loomed closer. He didn't notice the sheer drop that could have been the end of the world, and would have been the end of him if he had fallen. Instead he flounced toward the precipice with a wide smile upon his face.

I am free, I am excited, I am filled with joy. Let my spiritual quest begin!

These were the thoughts that played like a mantra in his head, and like any magical chant, the words held a power of their own, a power so potent that it was enough to launch him off his feet. He lifted up into the air, closed his eyes and flew. Like a feather floating lazily on a gentle breeze, he drifted up, up, and away, with all his dreams intact.

If anyone had witnessed the spectacle besides the little dog, they would no doubt say it was magic and perhaps it was, for the Fool had a magic running deep within his soul that he didn't even know about.

Like any hapless child, he was unaware of his true nature and the things he could manifest.

As it was, he was on his own in a land of dreams and about to learn the secrets of the Universe. Tossing and turning as the wind picked up, the Fool never opened his eyes. He had complete trust that all would work out as it should, that he would eventually find his feet and be able to move on.

Gradually as the breeze settled, so too did the Fool, his soles grazing the dusty ground beneath. Once more he was standing upright, with the earth to support him. Taking a deep breath, he opened his eyes and surveyed the landscape. The vista before him was full of potential; a blank canvas from which he could create anything. The town of his birth was gone, the mountains too. Everything was different and new. It was now he realized; the moment had come.

His quest had at last begun!

The Fool card marks the beginning of a new cycle or journey. Keep your head up, and step boldly into the future!

THE MAGICIAN.

1 THE MAGICIAN

THEMES

Manifestation

Inspired action

Creative impulses

Power

THE FIRST PERSON THE FOOL ENCOUNTERED when he arrived in this new world was the Magician. It took him a moment to find his balance and adjust his vision. Squinting, he could make out a great expanse of sand. He initially thought he was alone, a stranger lost in time and although that did not bother the Fool, he wondered what his next step might be. What was his intention, and what did he wish to create? Surely that was why he was here standing in the middle of a vast nothingness.

He looked in every direction. All he could see was a deserted stretch of white that rose up to meet the bluest sky, but then something strange happened. The air before him began to shimmer. Slithers of sunlight blinded him, if only for a second and, when he rubbed his eyes, the view had changed.

Ruby-red flowers and lush green foliage curled about his feet and, wherever he gazed, more grew. It was as if the power of his stare was the catalyst, the cause for this strange phenomenon. Before him was a table laden with objects that made no sense on first appearance, and behind the table stood a man of such magnificence, the Fool could hardly tear his eyes away.

The man was dressed in a white robe for purity, with a blood-red cloak draped around his shoulders. Gripping him tightly about the waist was a silvery snake biting its own tail. The Fool recognized this as a symbol of eternal life, and the ongoing cycles that every human moves through.

Silence hung in the air between them; it was as if nothing else existed in this moment; nothing except the relationship between the two. The Fool took a step forward. He could feel the aura of this powerful man drawing him close.

"Who are you?" he asked, and the tall man spoke into his head.

"I am the Magician; I am the master of my own destiny, and these are the tools of my trade." And his gaze dropped to the table, to the cup and pentacle, the sword and wand, which lay upon the surface.

The Fool studied each one in turn. He looked at the shape of the cup; it was more than a drinking vessel, it held the elixir of life, the purest, sweetest water to touch his lips. Then he studied the pentacle, shiny and gold, smooth to touch but born from earth—a symbol of material wealth. He studied the sword then, the sharp edge reflecting the sun's rays. Swift and smooth, it could slice through the air. Then finally he turned his attention to the wand. Like an arrow crafted from wood, it was the spark that lit the fire of new ideas. Finally he understood what the Magician meant. These tools represented the four essential elements for all creation—water, earth, air, and fire.

"I understand," he said, holding the gaze of the Magician. "These things are at my fingertips, and I can use them to create my future."

The Magician smiled, then slowly raised one hand toward the sky, the other toward the earth, in one fluid movement. Every action was done with intention, every placement so specific, there could be no doubt or questioning him. This was a man with a vision in mind.

The Fool watched and tried to understand once more what the Magician might be telling him. He scratched his head. He took a breath and let the cool air calm his thoughts. He realized that to learn, he must be like the cup; an open vessel ready to catch those drops of wisdom. To truly connect he must be like the pentacle, born from the earth and rooted in the physical. To stimulate his mind he must be like the sword, sharp and ready for action; and to understand, he must wield the wand that is primed to light the flame of knowledge. In that moment, the truth came to him, and he realized the significance of the Magician's hands and where they were pointing.

"You point to the heavens, to the spiritual realm, which we are all a part of," he said, looking upward and then dropping his gaze to the earth, "and you point to the earthly, material realm, to represent the physical. We stand with a foot in each, and it is up to us to find that balance as we move through life."

The Magician nodded as the revelation settled in the Fool's mind.

Then out of nowhere the Fool spoke once more.

"Why can I only hear you in my head? Why do you not speak to me out loud?"

The Magician seemed amused by this question, although he did not laugh. A flicker of emotion passed across his face that made his lips twitch, then he did something that the Fool did not expect.

He stepped forward and in one graceful stride, slipped like a shadow over the sun, into the Fool. Suddenly he was gone, and the Fool understood everything. The Magician was not a separate entity; he *was* the Fool. He was the next stage in his development.

"I am you, and you are me," the Fool said triumphantly. "You are the outer representation of all that I can achieve!"

He grinned as the wisdom consumed him.

"I have the power to manifest. I have all of the tools at my fingertips." He clicked his fingers and watched as the blooms at his feet multiplied.

"To shape my reality, I must ensure my dreams and goals are rooted in both the spiritual and material realms." The Fool paused. "I understand, and I am ready for my next lesson."

His statement was met with a second of silence, and once more the vista transformed. In the blink of an eye the foliage disappeared, as did all the Magician's tools. The ground beneath his feet hardened and the vast stretch of desert was gone. The air seemed to pulsate with energy, and the Fool gripped his head in his hands. Whatever was coming had the power to shake his foundations to the core. The sky darkened, and the Fool was cast into a spectral half-light.

The Magician calls you to step into your power.
You have all you need to make your dreams
come true. Now is the time to manifest.

THE HIGH PRIESTESS

2 THE HIGH PRIESTESS

THE GROUND BECKONED; THE FOOL felt himself crumble and coil into a small ball. He closed his eyes, and in that one motion opened up to his subconscious mind, for while he couldn't see what was happening, he could sense it inside. As the dim light grew, the shade offered a moment of introspection and the Fool looked inward. He realized that while the Magician represented power in a conscious masculine way, there needed to be a balance. Slowly, steadily as he rose to his feet and opened his eyes, he witnessed the changes.

Before him was the entrance to a stone temple; sitting in his path was a beautiful woman draped in the softest blue robes. Behind her hung a veil daubed with a pomegranate pattern, a symbol of the Greek goddess Persephone and her link to the Underworld. He realized then that this was the entrance to his subconscious mind and the being before him symbolized divine feminine energy.

When their eyes met it was as if time stood still. There was no breath, no heartbeat, not a single sound or motion, as they connected at a deep soul level. The High Priestess, for that is what she was, stared and her gaze posed a question in the Fool's mind—*What hidden parts of me do I need to acknowledge in order to move forward?*

Wearing a horned diadem as a symbol of her divine knowledge, and holding a scroll with the letters TORA scribed upon it to represent the Greater Law, the High Priestess sat in stillness. With an aura of serenity she beckoned the Fool closer, and it was as if he no longer had control of any part of his body. It seemed that he was gliding in a spectral dance toward the temple, unable to resist or do anything except connect with the unknown.

He wondered as he floated if this was what happened when you drifted from slumber into dream; was there nothing you could do except surrender to the deeper recesses of your subconscious mind? It seemed fitting that the landscape had taken on a dreamlike appearance to the Fool, and he would have smiled if he'd been fully in control of his expressions.

Eventually he found himself face to face with the High Priestess, locked into her gaze. He wondered if she was reading his mind, probing the depths with razor-like precision. Her face was beatific; peaceful, hopeful, and wise; the Fool let this energy wash over him.

Gently she turned her head, first to the black pillar and then to the white, as if drawing his attention to their differences.

"I don't understand," the Fool said, finally finding he had a voice.

"See," she whispered, and once more turned her head in either direction. This time, he noticed the letters etched upon each column. B on the black pillar, signifying Boaz, meaning "in his strength" and J on the white pillar to represent Jachin, meaning "he will establish." Dual and opposing, the same but different—together they held the temple securely in place; each one equally important.

The Fool nodded, and felt her grip released. He stood before her now of his own free will. He no longer questioned what he might find within the temple of his own mind. Yes, there were shadowy secrets; things that he might hide from others, but not from himself. To truly master his magic he needed to acknowledge both the light and the dark, the male and female energy at work within him.

He looked then to her feet and noticed the crescent moon nestled there. It sparkled with a brightness he had never seen before.

"What does this mean?" he asked, and in that moment a vision came into his mind.

The Fool saw the moon, full and fat in the night sky, casting a glow upon the land. It was brimming with potential and power. Then ever so slowly it reduced in size, fading to the crescent shape that he recognized. He also felt the same waning in his soul, as if he was letting go of things that he no longer needed in his life. As the moon became invisible, he too became absorbed by darkness, cushioned, and protected in the black velvety sky. Slowly the moon emerged again, growing from a delicate crescent form to a full round orb of light. Within him he felt the flame of inspiration grow as ideas sprang forth, and he swelled with creativity.

"I understand." He smiled. "The cycles of the moon impact upon us; they match the continuing cycles that we go through, and we can connect with lunar energy to help us, but we must do it intuitively."

Closing his eyes, the Fool turned his attention inward to the beating of his heart and to the rise and fall of his chest. He focused on each breath, on drawing the air deep from the soles of his feet, and letting it flood his body. He relaxed, and released his outward breath, letting it seep from his lips into the atmosphere. The more attention he paid to this rhythmic breathing cycle, the more his intuition developed. As this grew, he began to drift forward, passing between the stone pillars and floating through the entrance of the temple. He flowed effortlessly into the main chamber where the sacred knowledge of the Ancients could be found. This was the seat of his subconscious mind, the place where he would find all of the answers to all of the questions that would ever arise in his lifetime. He rested there for a moment, comfortable in the space and open to any insights. He recognized that now he had found this inner temple, he would always be able to come back to it, to retreat from the world and seek solitude and peace within this sanctuary. This thought gave him great comfort.

Just as the Fool was getting used to the idea of languishing in the safety of his subconscious forever, the walls came crashing down. The ceiling became the ground beneath his feet, and everything turned on its head.

The High Priestess invites you to embrace your feminine power. Trust your intuition and know that you have the answers within.

III

THE EMPRESS.

3 THE EMPRESS

THEMES

Nurturing energy

Femininity

Beauty

Nature's abundance

THE FOOL WAS CONFUSED; he had not expected to be thrust into another vista so soon. He had supposed that he had found an escape, a place he could stay and be at one with his thoughts. Instead everything was changing, the temple was gone, the desert vanished, the burnished sky and blazing sun replaced by a softer backdrop.

Fluffy white clouds floated above the Fool's head, and beneath his feet the ground was pliable and warm. A carpet of grass had sprung from nowhere, stretching in every direction, and as he looked he could see dips and mounds form in the distance. Hills and valleys rippled into existence before his eyes. The earth was verdant and rich; the soil was fertile. He turned around and found that he was standing in the middle of a giant wildflower meadow. Tiny buds and flower heads peeked from between the damp grasses; pretty pinks and jewel-like reds, sunshine yellows, and the brightest blues gathered at his feet, and in that moment he felt like a King. Behind him a forest appeared, thick swarthy trees towered and formed the canopy, and then sweeping around and down, a sparkling freshwater stream. He watched as it swept past him.

Where am I? wondered the Fool and, as if in answer, the landscape pulsated, matching the rise and fall of his chest. A feeling of security came over him, as if he had been in this place before. It felt like home, and he relaxed and marveled at the beauty of his surroundings.

From behind him came a voice, soft and mellow like it was born from the earth.

"My son," it said and, as the Fool spun around, the voice came into being, melding from the land and taking the shape of a voluptuous woman seated on an array of cushions.

"Mother," the Fool said, without even thinking. The word dripped from his tongue and hung in the air between them.

The woman had golden hair, and a flowing robe adorned with pomegranates to represent her fertility. She looked majestic, like a bountiful Empress surveying her kingdom and all that it encompassed. There was an air of peace about her, as if her presence could calm a raging storm and bring sunshine to the darkest day. She did not move or offer any more, and the Fool did not ask. Falling beneath her gaze was like being wrapped up in the softest, warmest blanket, and that was enough.

In that moment the Fool felt totally loved and nurtured. He knew that he belonged, not only to this woman, but also to the earth. He was as much a part of nature as the new shoots that burst through the soil and sought the light of the sun. He felt vibrant, alive, and connected in every way.

The Empress smiled and in that one expression the Fool understood why he could not stay in the realm of the subconscious forever. It was his purpose to journey through life, to see, feel, and experience the world around him, to engage all of his senses, and move amongst the natural world, rather than being separate from it.

"There is a place and a purpose for everything," the Empress whispered, and the Fool agreed.

"Everything in balance," said the Fool, and it was then that he noticed the twinkling stars she wore as a crown upon her head. There were twelve, to represent the twelve months of the year, and the planets in the sky; a celestial celebration of the Universe, and a way of showing her connection to the passing seasons. It was a connection he also felt in his soul. He was more than just flesh and bones; his spirit was born from the cosmos and moved within him.

The Fool sat on the ground at the feet of the Empress and gazed up adoringly. She was both mother and leader, a powerful, caring energy and he didn't want to leave this place. It was moment of respite, a time to recharge, to evaluate what he had learned so far and what he still needed to find on his journey. There was comfort here, too, the kind of nourishment that every child needs in order to grow. Eventually after what could have been minutes, hours, or even weeks, for the

Fool could not tell how time worked in this otherworldly space, he gathered his strength and rose.

"I must go; there is more for me to discover but I do not want to leave you."

The Empress smiled. "I am never far away, I am always with you."

The Fool was puzzled. "How can this be?"

"I am the breeze that kisses your face, the earth that caresses your feet as you walk. I am the leaves that hang from the branches and ruffle your hair. I am the flowers that catch your eye and capture your imagination with their sweet scent. I am all things because I am Mother Nature."

The Fool nodded. "So wherever I go, you are always there. All I have to do is reach out."

"Yes," the Empress said. "Connect with your heart and soul, and your senses, and you will feel me. Whenever you need to replenish the soul, to heal and forgive, then connect with my power."

And so it was that the Fool once more stepped out on his own, leaving the safety and security of the Empress and venturing forth into the unknown. He did not wait for the vista to catapult him into a new scenario; instead he took control and took the path that led into the woods. Each footstep was purposeful, each breath deep and energizing. He was a young man on a mission, who had grown from his experiences so far. He did not look back, for there was only one way to go. His adventure had just begun, and already he could feel the changes at work within him.

"Onward and upward!" he said, with passion.

The Empress signals a creative period.
Nurture your interests and let your creativity flow.
A mother figure in your life is there to help you.

THE EMPEROR.

4 THE EMPEROR

THEMES

Authority

Rules

Structure

Father figure

THE WOOD THAT THE FOOL HAD SEEN IN THE DISTANCE when he sat with the Empress was more like a forest close up, with dense, thick vegetation, trees that seemed to go on forever, and a mossy, dark interior. While he wasn't normally governed by fear, there was something off-putting about this place, as if stepping inside might put him at risk. Even so, the Fool blundered onward. He longed to know what was on the other side of the forest. Taking the only path he could find, he ambled through the trees, twisting and turning as if he was navigating a labyrinth.

Perhaps he should have trusted his intuition, for there was something forbidden here, but being the Fool he paid no attention to his sixth sense and the warnings that played through his mind. Now that he was inside there was nothing more to do, except keep walking and ignore the strange rustling, snuffling sounds that seemed to be chasing his every step. In the distance he heard a shrill howling noise, which made him jump and propelled him forward even faster. Soon he was running, sweeping through the trees at such a pace that the branches were clawing at his skin. It was dark and he couldn't see anything in front of him. As his foot hit a rock his ankle twisted, and he lost his balance completely. Tumbling through the forest floor, he finally came to a halt on what felt like flat ground.

He looked up and realized the reason he had come to a standstill was thanks to an enormous stone throne standing in his path. The seat was adorned with four rams' heads, a symbol associated with the warrior planet Mars. As he studied the etchings, he became aware that he, too, was being watched. A man of senior years with a long white beard and a regal appearance was seated in the giant chair. He wore a gold crown upon his head, making it immediately obvious that this was the Emperor. His stern expression wasn't without kindness; there was concern etched into the lines of his face.

The Fool tried to stand but his sore ankle made him stumble, so he crouched on a patch of dirt.

"Sir, I am sorry for this intrusion."

"I am the Emperor, and I am here to teach you a valuable life lesson," the man said. His voice had the timbre of an ancient oak— mighty and strong.

The Fool flinched, and instinctively moved backward as the Emperor continued his speech.

"Your instincts told you not to enter the forest, but you plowed ahead, ignoring the warnings in here," and he tapped his chest, "without thought for much else except your own curiosity. You did not anticipate what might happen if you got lost, or what else might lurk in the hidden depths."

The Fool nodded. "I only thought about what I wanted."

The Emperor lent forward. "And that is the mistake you made. There are rules in life that must be followed. We might not always agree with them, but they keep us safe and help us upon the path." He paused, and then looked into the distance. "Have you not learned to trust your intuition?"

The Fool stared at the ground; trailing a hand over the soil he felt the warmth of Mother Earth soothing him.

"I need to think more carefully," he said at last. "I should have trusted my instincts and listened to what they were telling me instead of blindly forging ahead."

Raising his face, he looked at the Emperor, who was holding in one hand an Egyptian Ankh, a symbol of protection and strength, and an orb in the other to represent the world he governed. Suddenly the connection between the two was clear. While the Emperor was an authority figure, he was also a father who cared and wanted the best for his children. His manner might appear somber, but it was for good reason that acted in this way. He took his responsibility seriously and sought to offer protection and strength to those who needed it.

"There will be times in life when you need to be like me, the Emperor of your own world. You need to operate within a framework and follow certain laws to protect yourself and others. There will also be times when you can be the Fool, and act impulsively and without judgment. The lesson is in knowing who you need to be at any given time."

The Fool listened intently to the advice. He couldn't fail to be mesmerized by such a powerful presence. When the Emperor had finished talking, the Fool took a moment to digest all he had said and look at his surroundings. In the distance, rising up behind the stone throne, he could see a vast mountain range. Peaks and troughs made a jagged pattern across the red sky, and the forest from earlier was gone. The bright backdrop matched the color of the Emperor's robes, and denoted an aura of greatness and a forceful energy. This was a man who could not be ignored.

Gradually the Fool stood up, but the pain in his ankle made him wince. He could put no weight upon his foot, and he stumbled once more. The Emperor held out a hand, and steadied him.

"It's time for you to go, to continue your quest."

The Fool nodded but looked down at his ruined ankle and wondered how he would fare crossing the mountains.

The Emperor pointed the Ankh toward the Fool's foot, sending a ray of healing light in its direction. Instantly there was a warmth, as the tendons inside repaired and the muscle was once more strong.

"Go, be safe. Remember what I have told you," the Emperor said. "You do not know it all. Be open to the lessons of others."

"I will heed your wise words," said the Fool. His enthusiasm had returned once more. He felt stronger than ever and was ready for the next stage in his journey.

The Emperor exudes authority.
Consider how you can embrace the role
of father figure for others.

V

THE HIEROPHANT

5 THE HIEROPHANT

Spiritual wisdom

Religious beliefs

Conformity

Ancient knowledge

THE FOOL TRAVELED ON WITH HOPE IN HIS HEART and an open mind. He had already learned so much about himself and his potential, but he wanted to know more about the world and how it worked. Before he could come to any conclusions, he needed to know what others believed, and if there was some kind of spiritual order to things. Should he live by a set of values, and if so, who decided these? Or would it be better to follow his own intuitive urges? As he pondered these issues the Fool climbed higher and farther than he had ever been before. He had been traveling for some days, although it was hard to know exactly how long.

The mountain range was treacherous and not for the unskilled, but the Fool seemed to have a knack for navigating and found he could work his way across by using the clefts and crevices as footholds. Finally, he reached the other side and could see a collection of buildings in the valley below. It looked like a small town, and that excited him, for there would surely be people there to learn from.

He clambered down the mountain with the wind at his heels, and soon reached solid ground. Just ahead he saw the city gates and followed the white stone path toward the central square. It seemed deserted, as if all of the people had fled at the same time. While he was seeking company, he was also curious about his surroundings, so he decided to explore. The building that intrigued him the most was the small white temple that stood higher than the rest of the structures. Slowly he mounted the path to the entrance and, as he got closer, he saw three figures clustered together.

The main figure was a man, who was raised up and seated on an ornate throne between the two main pillars. Below him, bending at his feet, were two people; their faces seemed to be pressed against the stone floor, their hands clasped together.

How strange! thought the Fool. *What can they be doing? Is this some sort of worship, or perhaps a ritual?*

He had to know more.

On reaching the scene, the Fool hesitated. He did not wish to interrupt. He remembered the wise words of the Emperor, and how it was best not to rush headfirst into everything. Taking a step backward he watched, as the imposing figure with the three-tiered crown issued words of reassurance and comfort upon the gathered pair. While waiting to be summoned, he focused his attention on the man's appearance. Wearing three robes—one blue, one white, and one red, just like his triple crown—it became clear that this was to signify the three realms over which he ruled: the conscious; the sub-conscious; and the super conscious, the universal realm of spirit where all thoughts are connected. It also made the Fool think of three aspects, or states of being, such as birth, life, and death; or past, present, and future. This was certainly a deeply religious and learned man and he longed to know what was at the heart of his teachings.

His right hand was raised as if blessing the two followers at his feet, but on closer inspection the Fool could see that two fingers were pointing upward to the heavens and the spiritual realm, and two were pointing down toward the earth and the material realm.

Aha! the Fool thought. *He is encompassing both worlds and bringing the blessings of each upon them. This must surely be the Hierophant, a holy and knowledgeable man, a sage from whom I can learn great things.*

At that moment the Hierophant looked straight ahead and spoke to the Fool.

"Stranger, you are welcome to stay here for a while and learn from me. I can teach you about religion and tradition. I can reveal ancient truths and offer some understanding, but the final choice will be yours. How you see the world and what you believe is entirely up to you."

The Fool let these words sink into his mind. He was ready to be guided in this way, to receive this knowledge. He walked forward and bent at the knee like the other followers.

"Teach me master, I will be a willing student."

And so it was that the Fool stayed for many days in the company of the Hierophant. Each religious doctrine he studied with diligence, and performed the rites and rituals associated with that tradition in order to gain a deeper insight and take meaning from his lessons. He listened and he learned. He discovered the art of prayer, and how to perform this simple ritual to help and heal. He asked many questions, and the Hierophant was always happy to answer, to offer advice or a theory behind the working of each principle. In return, the Fool led a modest life. He slept in one of the stone rooms at the back of the temple. He served the Hierophant, making meals and cleaning the place of worship as part of his board. He didn't miss the excitement of travel because he found a different kind of joy in the structure of each day, and the wisdom that he took to heart. He remembered all he had experienced so far during his quest; his meetings with the Magician and the High Priestess, spending time with Mother Earth in the guise of the bountiful Empress, and learning about authority and rules from the impressive Emperor.

Finally, one day, he knew that his time with the Hierophant had come to an end. He couldn't say how he knew, for it came to him intuitively and, as with all things during this venture, he felt the urge to move once more, to explore and see what was on offer.

He packed his knapsack and spent some silent time in prayer, giving thanks for every piece of knowledge he had been given. Then, when the moon was high in the sky, casting its luminescence on the Earth below, the Fool said his goodbyes and made his way down the stone path, away from the small town and off into the distance.

The Hierophant asks you to address
your spiritual beliefs. Seek knowledge and
wisdom from those you trust.

THE LOVERS.

6 THE LOVERS

THEMES

Love

Relationships

Decisions

The choice between
two paths

THE FOOL WALKED LONG INTO THE NIGHT, and the dawn of the following day. He walked uphill, and down, following the undulating curves of each valley. He took long, graceful strides, and counted time in his head. Hearing his own voice kept him company, for he lacked any real association. His little white dog was long since gone, for when he stepped off the cliff it had been a solitary endeavor, a path that only he could take.

While he loved the freedom of being on his own, he felt a stirring for something new and realized that some part of him craved human affection. The bond that he had seen in so many was something that had eluded him, most likely because he wasn't ready for that kind of connection. But after months of travel and learning, it seemed that a yearning had grown deep within, and he was ready to make that choice.

As the sun flooded the sky with golden warmth, the Fool found himself standing in a beautiful garden, surrounded by fruit trees. It was a glorious place, almost heavenly in appearance. Rich, vibrant greens were met with bright, berry red fruits, and blossom of every color. Suddenly he felt the urge to experience this place freely without being encumbered, to feel the sun upon his naked skin and absorb its energizing rays.

He rid himself of all clothing and cast aside his baggage, then stood, face turned upward, eyes closed. To breathe in the moment, to be in the moment, the Fool felt elated! After a few minutes of simply enjoying the peace, he felt another presence, someone close by. Slowly he dropped his gaze and looked about him.

The woman stood resplendent and, just like the Fool, she seemed lost in the moment, caught in the pleasure of being in this wondrous place. Her long hair trailed over her shoulders and every curve and sinew could be seen. The Fool breathed her in. He longed to reach out and touch her, to feel the gentle warmth of her smooth skin against his. These emotions were new to him, but they did not feel alien. Instead the Fool felt an anticipation he had not experienced before.

Behind her, he noticed an apple tree laden with fruit ripe for the picking. What a gift! What a joy! It seemed he really was in heaven, except that there was something else there too, slithering slowly and winding its way around the trunk—a snake with silvery skin and a forked tongue, a serpent amidst the beauty, ready to catch him unawares. He had seen this snake somewhere before. He pored through the recesses of his mind, and the recent teachings he had received, until he found what he needed—the Garden of Eden and the temptation of Adam and Eve. He remembered the story well, and now he was living it for himself, facing a similar choice.

It was then that the Fool became aware of an intense crackling heat and he turned to find a tree of flames behind him. Flickering tendrils of fire stretched from the branches, like orange leaves. The Fool longed to touch one, to feel the searing warmth against the palm of his hand, but it was a foolish thought and one weighted by passion.

He realized then that this new chapter of his story was about the choice between two paths and making the right decision at the right time. Should he try and capture the flame, or let it be, and what would be the consequence of this action? Should he let desire consume him, and form a loving union with this woman, or walk away and take a different path? Would his heart rule his head, or would he make a more reasoned choice? The Fool wondered how he was supposed to know what was right, for surely love in itself was a good thing. There were, after all, many different kinds of love to experience.

As if in answer to his silent question, an Angel emerged from the clouds that had gathered above their heads. The Fool held his breath. He had never seen such a magnificent being before. With enormous ruby-red wings that seemed to go on forever, the Angel shimmered with light.

Taking a deep breath, the Fool asked, "How do I know which choice is right for me?"

The Angel didn't answer directly, but the Fool could sense a sudden shift in his understanding. The confusion from earlier had cleared, and there was a reassuring warmth in his heart.

It all starts and ends with love, he thought, *and every decision, if made with love, is the right choice at the time. I must follow my heart and love myself—that is the key. It may take me away from here and down a new path, but I must be true to myself.*

The Fool opened his arms wide to embrace the emotion fully. He realized in that moment that there were so many different types of love, from the physical, between two people, to self-love and the spiritual, and they were all possible for him.

The evening crept in slowly, the bright sunlight fading to a soft amber glow, and it was time for the Fool to go, to leave this heavenly place and step out into the world once more. This time, however, he had grown even more. There was a physical blossoming; he had found his feet, a strengthening of his resolve, and a deeper bliss and understanding that lived within his heart. He knew something of the divine joy of love, and what it was to revel in this emotion. He had taken charge of his destiny and made a decision based on how he felt at the time. Before this moment he would surely have let fate decide, but now he was in control. He was the driving force in his life.

Clothed and ready to face any challenge, the Fool left the confines of the garden behind him. He didn't look back, because his thoughts were very much directed toward the future, and he had no regrets. He had chosen to leave and take this path, and that was all he needed to know.

*The Lovers card shows that love is
on your mind. A decision must be made;
be open and follow your heart.*

THE CHARIOT.

7 THE CHARIOT

THEMES

Willpower

Focused action

Control

Determination

THE FOOL HAD NOT FELT TIRED since the start of his journey. It seemed that every step imbued him with energy and helped to propel him forward. He was driven and infused with vitality. Even when covering hard, rugged terrain, his feet would spring lightly and land in the perfect position. Some might say the gods were with him, but the Fool recognized that this determination to move forward came from his inner core and the experiences he'd had along the way. Treading the path was just as important as reaching the destination, for it was during the journey that he would find himself.

Even so, when the Fool stumbled upon a discarded Chariot by the side of the road, he couldn't believe his luck. It seemed like an open invitation, as if destiny was working in his favor. The Chariot itself was plush and regal, the kind of vehicle fit for a King. With a canopy of stars that hung down from the roof, it was a celestial vision and one that the Fool could not resist. With a vehicle such as this he could make great progress if he only knew how to drive it!

On closer inspection, the Fool noticed a set of armor laid carefully upon the seat. Crescent moons adorned each shoulder to represent the future and what would come to pass, and there upon the breast plate, a single, solid square—the alchemical symbol for "strength of will." The Fool pondered if this was a clue to the Chariot's source of power. The armor was sparkling, and felt like it had never been worn before, another sign that it was meant for him. It was fate that he should don the apparel and take his place at the Chariot's helm.

Quickly he changed. The armor was the perfect fit; wearing it, he felt a sense of authority and was more motivated than before. It was then that he noticed the wand, which was also on the seat. The Fool knew of magic from his encounter with the Magician, but he had never used a magical tool. Again, he felt compelled to reach out, to scoop up the wand and hold it in his fingertips. How wonderful it felt, as it nestled in his hand. The cool wood sent an icy tingle along his arm, which snaked around his neck and shoulders, and settled in the center of his chest. For every breath in, he felt the prickle of enchantment spread, and for every breath out, he could sense his energy expanding.

At the front of the Chariot, sitting so patiently that they almost looked like statues, were one black and one white sphinx. Polar opposites, they crouched facing different directions, but in every other way they were identical.

Balance, thought the Fool, *just like the black and white pillars of the High Priestess's temple, these two opposing forces can find a common ground and purpose, if they work together.*

It seemed that all of the teachings he had mastered so far were now making sense. Everything was coming together as it should, in order for him to make progress in his quest.

But how do I drive the Chariot? probed the Fool, for there were no reins to steer or motivate, nothing to hold on to. It seemed that the Chariot was missing something but the Fool couldn't work out what it was.

He climbed inside and stood at the front looking out. Ahead, he could see where he wanted to be. The landscape was calling to him, and there was much to do. It was the time to take action, to focus and direct his will, and yet "where to" and "how" were the big questions. The Fool felt clueless, and then he remembered the wise words of the High Priestess. She had told him that he had all of the answers he needed within.

Taking a deep breath, he drew his attention once more to that interior world, to the seat of his power. He drew his energy from this place and directed his will, but this time he focused on the Chariot moving. He saw in his mind where he wanted to be, pictured it as clearly as he could and, with all his might, wished it into being. Slowly, the sphinx began to stir and there was a deep rumbling sound as the wheels of the Chariot turned. It was moving forward!

It was then that he realized he still had the wand in his grip. Raising it in his hand, he stood tall and leaned forward, pushed all his power through the wand and sent a clear intention out into the world. Without words, for words were not needed at this time, he urged the Chariot onward, and this time it moved faster, stronger, the wheels clattering forward at such a speed it took the Fool by surprise.

As the view sped past him, and the Chariot covered more ground, the Fool felt a sense of achievement. He had made it work; he was in control. If he could apply himself in this way at all times, then he would surely make a success of his life. This knowledge thrust him forward. He felt inspired and ready for anything.

"Now is the time to be bold," he shouted, "to make my way in the world, and set my sights on the future!"

He did not know yet what that future might hold, but he was feeling optimistic. The path ahead traveled between the mountains, but there was nothing more to see except a dusty road. The unknown didn't bother the Fool. He was determined to plow onward, to maintain the force and fervor that he felt in his belly.

Once more he drew strength from within, and focused on the wheels of the Chariot, and the sphinx that pulled it. He drew them together in his mind, each one working individually, but making the perfect team. He visualized the journey and unleashed his will with a fiery steel that could not be ignored.

The Chariot urges you to draw upon your willpower and stay focused. Take positive action, and you will reap the rewards!

8 STRENGTH

THEMES

Inner strength

Resilience

Persuasion

A calm manner

THE FOOL HAD TRAVELED MANY MILES upon the Chariot, but the landscape was changing, and the dusty paths were now rocky and uneven. The brittle surface made it difficult for the wheels to roll, and so in the end the Fool conceded and left the Chariot behind. He knew that he was heading in the right direction and that, somehow, he would need to cross this terrain. Ever determined, he plowed on, trudging and climbing, carefully planting each foot where he could. The sun was unforgiving above his head, and he felt the full weight of its heat press down on him. Despite his tenacity, he was growing weary, and his steps became more labored because of this. Sweat dripped from his brow and he licked his lips. How he longed for some respite, for a rock pool or a sparkling stream from which he could drink and refresh himself, but it was not meant to be.

Rising to the top of a small clump of rocks, he was caught by surprise. There was an enormous beast standing in his path. The Fool recognized this King of the jungle, and would have bowed low, but the lion issued an almighty roar that nearly knocked him off his feet. The creature's jaws snapped open, to reveal a row of teeth like jagged knives. The Fool felt fear rise up from his belly. He had never been in a situation like this before and was unsure how to act. He had nothing but his bare hands to fight the animal and would surely fall to his doom if it came to that. The lion was massive: a giant cloaked in fur the color of the setting sun. Against the backdrop of the mountains he was an impressive sight, and had it not been for the imminent threat, the Fool would have appreciated this moment much more. As it was, he stood motionless. He hardly dared breathe in case the noise should annoy this fearsome predator.

The Fool thought back to his previous experiences, and what they had taught him, but he could find no clue as to how to deal with the lion.

I cannot give up, he thought. *I have come too far to stop now, but my physical strength will not help me in this situation. I need something more.*

The lion took a step forward, every muscle in its body flexed. It was primed and ready to pounce. The Fool froze. He could not run; the lion would catch him in an instant. Could he play dead? No, this creature was clever, and would have its fun with him, before devouring him for his dinner. There was only one thing the Fool could do, and that was call upon the ancient teachings of the Hierophant and pray to some unseen force to save him.

At that moment, as if in answer to his prayer, a young woman emerged from behind the lion. Where she came from, the Fool had no idea. It was like she stepped out of nowhere at his hour of need. Wearing a white gown and a crown of flowers, she was the picture of innocence; a flower maiden imbued with the purest essence of nature. The Fool gasped as she gently took the lion's head into her hands and, uttering the softest, sweetest words, began to stroke her fingers through its mane and beneath its chin. Her loving gaze never left the lion's face, and she held firm with her hands, gripping and comforting the giant cat in her arms.

The Fool wanted to say something, to thank her for appearing out of nowhere and saving him from the jaws of death. He wanted to ask her how she had charmed the lion but he could find no words. Instead, he took a tentative step forward and opened his mouth.

"Sssshhh," the woman cooed, "let us keep the peace by using our inner strength. There is no need for brute force here."

By way of explanation, she looked into the Fool's eyes, and he felt the steely presence of her resolve.

"There are many types of strength that we can draw upon. Sometimes we need to endure, to find an inner resilience to help us move forward. It is not always about control in the physical sense. Look how the lion responds to my gentle touch. He does not fight because he does not see me as a threat. He senses that I am calm and strong, and so he feels calm and strong."

She smiled and that one expression lit up her face.

"When all else fails, learn how to go within and tap into those deep reserves, for resilience."

The Fool nodded. Again he tried to speak but found himself floundering, searching for a phrase that would not come.

The woman stood and stretched. She turned her face upward, closed her eyes and took a deep breath.

"We will leave you now to continue the rest of your journey. Go with strength, my friend."

Casually she turned in the opposite direction and, as if they were connected by an invisible cord, the lion also retreated, stepping in time with her gait. Steadily it sauntered away, as if it had never been there in the first place.

The Fool scratched his head. What had just happened? He wasn't sure, and yet he felt it was another lesson to absorb. He looked back in the direction he'd been going and realized there was still some way to go and a large stretch of rocky cliffs to navigate. He recalled the woman's words, how she'd mentioned resilience and the power to endure, to continue even when it seemed the world was against you.

"That is what I must do," he said quietly. "I cannot control my circumstance or change it, just as I could not control the lion. I simply need to draw upon my inner strength and move forward."

Drawing a deep breath to soothe his soul and slow his heart rate, he stepped out. Placing his feet firmly into the earth and feeling the dirt beneath, he pressed on. One step at a time, one foot in front of the other. Not giving in, not giving up, just being in the moment; composed, collected, and ready for whatever might come his way.

*The Strength card shows that you
have the confidence to overcome any obstacle.
Channel your emotions and face your fears.*

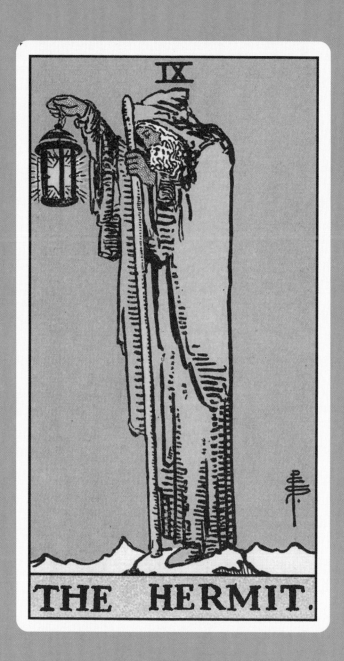

IX

THE HERMIT.

9 THE HERMIT

THE FOOL CONTINUED HIS JOURNEY ON FOOT for many days. It was tiring and arduous, but he would not stop. The quest meant everything to him, and each step he took brought him closer to fulfillment. It seemed that he had learned much from his venture, but the Fool knew there was more to come. He'd touched the tip of the mountain, but he had yet to go within, to succumb to the darkest parts within his psyche and reflect upon the true nature of life. For this he would need to take a different kind of journey, one that involved turning his attention inward. As with all things during this adventure, he knew that he had to wait until the time was right. There seemed to be an order, a pattern in which things happened, and each nugget of knowledge helped him move toward the next.

Soon the Fool found himself scaling a tall mountain. It was like none he'd ever climbed before. The rock was slippery, and it was hard to get a foothold. His fingers hurt as he ran them over the smooth surface in search of a crevice. His hands were sore and bleeding, and every inch of his body ached. The bright clothes he had donned for the journey were little more than dirty rags. His thick, curly hair was long and straggly, and a white beard adorned his face. It seemed, upon the surface, that he had aged and while that was true for the years had passed, his appearance was misleading. Inside his heart beat strong and loud, and his vision was true.

Hauling himself up the mountainside, the Fool eventually made it to the top, where he found a plateau of icy stone. Snow glistened from the peaks in the distance and a biting wind chilled him to the bone. The landscape was unforgiving; jagged slices of rock protruded from every corner, and all was covered with a thin layer of white. Icicles had formed and the ground was slick and treacherous.

What is the purpose of bringing me here? he thought, as he looked at his surroundings. *There is nowhere for me to go and nothing for me to see.*

He turned then and saw that in the wall of rock behind him, there was an opening; it was a cave with a light coming from within. The Fool crawled upon his hands and knees until he reached the mouth of the cave and, taking a deep breath, threw himself inside. The interior was small but roomy enough for him to stand up and turn around. It was dry and sheltered from the harsh conditions, and although it was not warm, it was a safe haven, a place where the Fool could rest and assess his situation. The light that he had seen came from a small lantern that someone must have left. Perhaps they too were going on the same journey. As the Fool picked it up, he noticed the six-pointed star inside. It was gleaming, sending darts of illumination in every direction. He recognized it instantly from his studies with the Hierophant. It was the Seal of Solomon, a symbol of great wisdom and reflection.

It was then that he also spotted a bundle of dark material in the corner of the cave. Lifting it with his free hand, he could see that it was made from thick woven wool and formed a gray cloak. Another gift from the one who went before. The Fool smiled. Perhaps he was meant to be in this place after all. Carefully he wrapped it around his shoulders and lifted the hood over his head. He felt safe, warm, and concealed from the rest of the world.

The shivers that had made his teeth chatter were now gone, as the dark folds of fabric enveloped him, like the cave that he stood in. Hidden from the outside he was able to draw his attention inward, to reflect upon his situation and where life might be taking him. He needed this retreat, this time away from everything.

And so it was that the Fool sat, and he let his mind wander. He followed the path of his thoughts and let them lead him into the deeper recesses of his consciousness. He pondered, without pushing for answers; he simply let them come as and when they wanted to. The Fool evaluated his life so far, and what it meant to him. He acknowledged all that he had done, and all that he had learned.

In his seclusion, he found time to meditate and identify what was really important to him. Finally, after many days of reflection, when he was fully recharged and ready to emerge from the cave, he did so with a sense of enlightenment. Stepping forward into the light, he breathed in the snow-capped vista.

In isolation the Fool had found solace, and he felt renewed. He might not know the path ahead, or what was waiting for him, but he did know himself and that was a blessing. He felt grateful for this time, for it had allowed him to contemplate his life, and measure his thoughts.

Looking about him he spotted something sticking out of the snow; it was a smooth, wooden shaft, which on further investigation proved to be a staff.

It must be another item left to help me on my way, he thought. *Well I will gladly take this gift, along with the others.*

Quickly he released it from the icy tomb and used it as a staff to lean upon. He held the lamp aloft so that he could see where he was stepping and pulled the cloak around him tightly. Now was the time to move on. He was ready for the next stage in his epic quest. Slowly he shuffled forward and, although the weather impeded his speed, there was a vitality in the way he held himself. The Fool was comfortable in his skin, confident in his abilities, and filled with self-belief.

The Hermit invites you to retreat and seek refuge in your inner world. Reflect, recharge, and value your alone time.

WHEEL of FORTUNE.

10 WHEEL OF FORTUNE

THEMES

Destiny

Cycles of life

Karma

Changing luck

ON ALIGHTING THE MOUNTAIN, the Fool found himself in a vast, green meadow. Down here the weather was different. The sun was shining, and the air was sweet with the scent of honeysuckle. The grass was damp and prickly to the touch, and he felt like he had walked into a spring scene.

How different everything appeared from this vantage point, and the Fool mused on this and what was ahead. It seemed that in a heartbeat his situation had changed. The harsh conditions he had experienced on the mountain top were a thing of the past and he had stepped into a new day.

Taking a moment to enjoy his new surroundings, the Fool sat down, crossed his legs, and leaned back. Turning his face upward, he inhaled the cool and refreshing air. He felt invigorated. It seemed that in a matter of days he had gone from feeling heavy and weighted down, to finding renewed peace. Now, in this moment, he felt different again. His heart was light, and his playful spirit emerged.

"How the wheel turns," he muttered to himself, for indeed it had and with a swiftness that had taken his breath away.

Then, as if to reinforce his words, the air above him shifted. A great whooshing sound could be heard, and the Fool shielded his eyes. Gradually the fluffy white clouds parted to reveal an astounding sight.

Hanging above his head was a giant wheel with strange inscriptions carved into it. The Fool gasped and rubbed his eyes.

This must be a dream, he thought, for he had never seen anything like it before. He gazed up at the peculiar apparition, trying to understand its meaning and why it had been presented to him.

The wheel itself was enormous and supported by three spiritual beings. The Fool recognized the first to be Anubis, the Egyptian god of the dead. The master of the Underworld rose up from beneath the wheel, as if to welcome the souls of the dead into his realm. The second, descending on the left side, was a snake and a representation of the Egyptian god of evil, Typhon. On the top, seated peacefully and looking beatific, was the sphinx, the symbol of strength and knowledge. Three different aspects, all with an influence upon the wheel and the direction in which it would turn. It seemed to the Fool that this suggested the random nature of fate, and how it could turn upon its head at any point.

The Fool noticed then four letters inscribed into the wheel's face: YHVH. He knew them to be the unpronounceable name of God—the all-seeing, all-knowing universal force that is forever present. On closer inspection, he could see other letters that spelt TORA, meaning "law" or Tarot.

The powerful nature of the Wheel of Fortune hit him. He understood that this vision was not sent lightly. It was here in his mind for him to absorb the true nature of all things, to know that destiny was a continual spinning cycle, where one could move from despair and poverty to joy and abundance. It seemed to the Fool that there was a time for everything, and that wherever you were upon the wheel, you should know that change was inevitable. Even in the darkest times, light and hope would be ahead, and when you felt on top of the world, the feeling of elation would not last forever. Therefore every moment was precious; every experience was of value.

The Fool smiled; this realization gave him some comfort and certainly matched his view of the world so far. During his journey he had faced many struggles, but he had also experienced happiness.

Around the wheel floated other elements equally as important as the wheel itself: an angel, an eagle, a lion, and a bull. The Fool pondered on their importance and realized from his spiritual teachings that they represented the fixed signs of the Zodiac. Each one held its place and position, hovering in mid-air—an essential part of the whole.

For a minute he let this knowledge settle in his brain. There was no need to rush, to force a conclusion, for the wheel itself was not solid. It was transparent, an image made of air and therefore any understanding would be the same. There was nothing conclusive here, just a selection of ideas and a way of approaching the twists and turns of life.

"It is better to take each day as it comes," said the Fool aloud. "Each state we move through is temporary, and that is just part of the process. This is what the wheel teaches us."

Feeling relaxed, the Fool let himself fall back onto the ground, stretching out with his hands behind his head and his legs crossed. He gazed up as the image of the Wheel of Fortune began to fade. He watched it go, not with longing or any other kind of emotion, for he realized it was simply another lesson. He let his body sink deeper into the damp grass, and let the ground support him. For every breath he took, he felt the energy of the earth permeate his being. He drew it up through his flesh and into his heart. Every time he exhaled, he let go of all that was troubling him. He released any worry or doubt back into the earth where it could be transformed into a positive energy. This was the cycle of life; in and out, round and round. On and on it would go till the end of time.

The Fool smiled; he was beginning to enjoy this quest, to see the pattern and to embrace every single part of the journey, but what next?

"Who knows!" he said, answering his own question. "Whatever is next, is next. Be it good or bad. Whether I am riding high amongst the stars, or slipping deep beneath the earth. Whatever my fate, I welcome it with open arms."

The Wheel of Fortune heralds change.
Embrace the twists and turns of fate and
expect the unexpected.

11 JUSTICE

AFTER TRAVELING FOR A FEW MORE DAYS, the Fool found himself in the middle of a vast walled kingdom. It was an industrious place, for everywhere he looked there was hustle, bustle, and movement. People crowded together, they walked with purpose, and they talked animatedly as they went about their daily business. The buildings and the wall that surrounded them were made from polished white stone, which reflected the light outward and gave the appearance that within this city all was bright and possible. It was a place of potential, a space where opportunity could present itself at any turn. The Fool was excited and felt that whatever lesson he learned here it would be one that served him well in the future.

He strode through the city gates and toward the main square. Here clusters of folk were gathered, shouting and raising their fists, perhaps at some injustice that had occurred. The Fool watched and wondered what could be bothering them but continued on his path toward the main building with the huge clock tower. He had no idea why, but it seemed to be calling to him.

As he got closer, he realized it was a type of courthouse, a place where laws were passed and sentences given to those who had committed a crime. It felt regal, as if the bricks that held it together were crafted from logic and reason. He stood on the main step looking up, and that's when he saw her; a statue, polished and painted, and seated in a large throne-like chair between two pillars. For a second he was reminded of the High Priestess from earlier in his journey, but this woman had a different expression upon her face. She was without judgment, and yet there was a question upon her lips, a query that could not be ignored. It was as if gazing into her eyes had the power to bring it to the surface and, once acknowledged, it must be answered.

The Fool felt that question keenly in his soul, but he did not know how to respond. Instead, he stared at the statue and marveled at her beauty. She was fearsome, charged, and ready to dispense justice. In her right hand she held a sword that was raised upward, the double edge a reference to the two sides of an argument. It was razor-like and deathly sharp, ready to cut through the detritus and make a swift, clean decision. In her other hand she held a set of scales, a symbol synonymous with justice and a reflection of her name. The scales were also a representation of balance and finding the right path between two opposing points of view.

The woman before him was both logical and intuitive, and the Fool could see that any decision she made would be based on both types of thinking. He noticed then her crown, with the small square at the center. The crown itself was strong with even edges, and the square in the middle was the focus of his attention. To him, this signified an ordered mind, with structure and the ability to organize information quickly; exactly what he'd expect from Justice. Her robes were ruby red, and peeping out beneath them was a small white shoe, a splash of innocence and purity against such a strong, vibrant color. Everything about her held meaning, and the Fool took this to heart.

He realized then why he had been pulled toward this place. It was time for him to account for his actions so far. Everything he had done up until this point would be judged, and while this might have seemed a daunting prospect, the Fool understood the reality of this. It was not for Justice to deliver any kind of punishment; it was simply her role to ascertain the truth, and to listen with compassion. He would need to be honest and distinguish between actions based on the greater good, and those that were self-serving. There was an element of karma here, and the Fool would need to understand the Universal Law—what goes around comes around. He recalled then the movement of the wheel, and how fate could change in a heartbeat; a revelation occurred. It seemed that even when you had no control of your circumstances, you could build positive karma, do good deeds, and ultimately be rewarded with fortune in the future.

"Everything is connected," he whispered.

The statue of Justice moved then; it was only a slight waver of an expression, but it seemed to the Fool that the woman's lips curled upward at the ends. The beginnings of a smile had taken root. She was more than a sculpture, or a reminder to be fair and adhere to the law; she was real in spirit.

"Of course!" He clapped his hands. Like every element of his journey so far, there was something magical about her. She had a lesson to impart, and the Fool was an eager pupil. Shuffling closer to her feet, he opened his arms wide.

"I am ready to answer your questions, to go within, and reveal the truth of my actions. I know I am accountable for every choice I have made, and I am prepared for the consequences of my actions."

The statue of Justice watched and waited, as the Fool continued.

"From here on in, I will always question my decisions and ask if they are for the greater good, or solely for my benefit. I will consider how my actions affect others, instead of blindly leaping ahead, without thought. I have learned an important lesson today, and one that will stay with me."

The Fool rose to his feet then, looked Justice directly in the eye, and said, "Thank you for helping me see the truth."

Turning on his heel, he strode out onto the steps and looked down at the city below. He watched the crowd of people still squabbling in the stone square and wondered what issue had them so vexed. He hoped in his heart that they would come to an understanding and realize that justice would be served, in one form or another. He prayed for peace, in the hope that they would see all sides of the story. Then he departed the city and set out on his quest once more.

The Justice card asks you to consider the impact of your decisions. Explore your truth, then make a stand for what you believe is right.

THE HANGED MAN.

12 THE HANGED MAN

THEMES

Surrender

Sacrifice

Stagnation

A pause

New perspectives

DURING HIS TIME IN THE WHITE STONE CITY, the Fool had heard of a secret garden filled with the most glorious flowers, and he knew that it was close by. To be surrounded by sweet and colorful blooms was exactly what he needed, and he couldn't wait to reach this heavenly place. As he skipped onward, he could see a wood in the distance. He would need to pass through here to reach the hidden garden. He gripped his knapsack tightly and took a deep breath. The wood itself was a cluster of tightly grouped trees. Some of them stood like spears in the ground, while others were small and wizened. There were tree stumps, and bushes, and the earth was covered by a thick layer of moss. It felt damp inside but the moisture was refreshing, and the cool air was soothing upon his skin. The Fool liked it here and, despite the darkness, he felt comfortable taking his time and meandering along the path.

A clearing came into view and the Fool could see that the space was marked by several sturdy oaks. There in the center, growing from the soil, was a tree shaped like a cross. Its branches were bent and gnarly and it looked like a sculpture. As the sun filtered through the canopy, he could see that it cast a spotlight on the tree as if to enhance its power.

"How strange," he muttered to himself and charged forward to get a closer look. It was then that his foot slipped on the damp leaves. A thick wire sprang up from nowhere and wrapped itself snugly around his ankle. Within seconds he was hoisted into the air, his body hanging limply upside down.

"Help!" he cried, to no one in particular, for the woods were completely deserted and miles away from the nearest town. "Help!" he tried again, but was met with a whisper of wind, and the faint sound of a crow cawing in the distance.

The tree creaked as it held his weight, and the Fool swung gently to and fro. This was not what he had expected to happen, and he wasn't happy. After all, he had big plans. He had hoped to reach the garden before sunset, but now he was stuck, trapped, and hanging by his foot in a most precarious situation. He soon realized that struggling only tightened the grip of the wire, making it more uncomfortable and causing him to weave from side to side.

He felt frustrated, but there was nothing he could do to manipulate his fate. He'd have to accept this change of plan. Fighting against the situation only made it worse. He remembered everything he had learned so far; to embrace change in whatever form it came, to think about the consequences of his actions and, in doing so, act mindfully. The Fool knew that he would have to sacrifice the secret garden in order to learn a new lesson here. There was nothing else he could do, except be the Hanged Man.

And so the Fool rested. He relaxed and accepted the situation. He didn't try and change it or even attempt to escape. He simply enjoyed the stillness of the moment. He discovered that hanging upside down gave him a new perspective on the world. He saw things that he wouldn't normally see. The forest floor became the sky above his head, and the sky became an endless deep blue sea. The blood flowed through his body, and every muscle and sinew felt alive. He gulped down the air and released all of his fear as he exhaled. He crossed his arms behind his back to form an inverted triangle shape; a symbol of unity, of the power of three, and the cycles of life. He contemplated his situation and what might happen next, and all the time the tree sustained him. It connected him to the natural world, and he was able to draw on its invigorating energy. The Fool understood that all he had to do was wait. Eventually the branch would break, and he would be returned to the earth, and able to continue on his way.

And so he waited, and he waited, and he watched the landscape change, and the wood grow brittle. He felt the leaves drop and a chilly blanket of air sweep through the trees. Just when he thought he might give up, the branch snapped, and he tumbled to the ground.

The Fool was free once more, but he was in no rush. The time he had spent suspended in mid-air had given him fresh insight.

He realized that perhaps he was heading in the wrong direction, and that maybe a new approach to his quest was needed. The Universe had wanted him to stop, to take some time out from his journey and be present with his thoughts.

"Everything happens for a reason," the Fool said. "I can see that now, just as I know everything is connected."

He realized too that he may never find the secret garden, but that didn't really matter. If he stumbled upon it, then it was a blessing, but if he didn't, then it wasn't meant to be.

"Maybe this is the secret garden I was meant to find!" he said, spinning around. "This is where I was meant to be all along."

Picking up his knapsack once more, the Fool ambled off in the direction he'd been going. No longer with a specific destination in mind, instead he would enjoy the journey. He would delight in each step and take joy from his surroundings.

The wood watched him go. The trees swayed and the branches and twigs leaned in his direction. The cross where he had been the Hanged Man remained at the center of the glade, lit by a shaft of sunlight. It stood tall and firm, a symbol of sacrifice and strength.

The Hanged Man asks you to surrender to the moment, pause, and take stock. To move forward, you must take time out.

DEATH.

13 DEATH

THEMES

Endings

Transition

Transformation

Leaving something behind

A s the Fool emerged from the wood, he found himself standing in the middle of a giant field. The land was flat and smooth, and he could see in every direction. To the far side, on the right, there was a woman kneeling by a body, with a small child close by. He could hear her wailing and watched as she crumpled to the ground. An elderly man dressed in ceremonial garb, a bishop, stood over them; his hands were closed in prayer and although his mouth was moving, the Fool couldn't tell what he was saying.

What had passed here and why was the woman weeping? Whose was the body on the ground? The Fool had many questions and while he didn't wish to intrude on the distressing scene, he couldn't leave either. Slowly, tentatively he moved toward them, in the hope that he could perhaps calm the situation.

Above him the sky darkened, and the Fool watched as thunder clouds rolled in the distance. There was a sense of foreboding about this place, as if he had stepped into a portrait of a tragedy, at the precise moment of destruction. Even so, he kept walking. It felt like he was needed to bear witness to the scene. He was within arm's reach of the woman when he heard the pummeling sound of hooves upon dirt and the soft approach of a horseman. The Fool gasped in shock at what he saw. Seated upon a handsome white steed was a figure dressed in dark armor, but the face and body were fleshless. This was a skeleton rider, Death itself.

For the first time since the beginning of his quest the Fool felt truly fearful. His heart was hammering in his chest, and he took a step back, anything to get far away from this gruesome character. And yet the Death before him seemed perfectly calm. There was no malice there. It was as if this event was inevitable, and in reality it was, for who can run from death? Not the man laid on the ground, nor the weeping woman or her child. Death is universal.

The Fool noticed his flag, the white rose upon a black background, a symbol of innocence, purity, and immortality. The message was clear; death in itself is not a bad thing. It is simply a rite of passage, as you move from one state of being to another. The rose had five petals, the number being synonymous with change, and this made sense to the Fool, for death was also about transformation. It was a transition and could be applied to almost any stage of life. He remembered then the teachings of the Wheel of Fortune, and how change can come at any point.

"Death is the same," he mused. "It can be a small death, as you leave something behind and start a new chapter, or something much bigger. It is part of the cycle of life, and as such we experience it all of the time."

He turned his attention then to the bishop, who was pleading desperately with the skeletal figure, begging for the lives of those before him. Death was speechless and, having no face, it was impossible to read his emotions.

"He cannot change things," the Fool said out of the blue.

The bishop turned to face him.

"I am sorry some things have to happen, but they should not be feared. Death is just another cycle that we encounter every day."

"And how do you know this?" asked the bishop.

"I can see it," the Fool replied, "and I have learned many things upon my travels. Each day is a 'death'—the old day fades away so that the new one can be born. It has to happen, because if it didn't, life would not continue."

The bishop thought for a moment and nodded.

In the distance the Fool watched a boat drift down the river. It reminded him of those mythical tales, where spirits of the dead were carried across a great sea, escorted to the next realm by a mysterious boatman. Perhaps that was what was happening here, but no one could see. Fear had clouded their judgment.

"Death is not the end," he said finally. "It is a new beginning."

He pointed then. "Look how the sun sets between those two

towers. Tomorrow it will be reborn. It will rise at dawn and light up the sky with its warmth. It may disappear from our view, but it is always present, just as the souls who leave us are always within our hearts."

The woman smiled then. It was a small expression that flickered across her face and, for a moment, the sadness was gone. She seemed to understand and accept what had passed.

Death looked from one to another, and his gaze finally settled on the Fool. Slowly he extended an arm and then pointed a bony finger in the opposite direction.

The Fool was being told to go, that it was not his time yet. Death had released him but would be back at some point in the future, of that he could be assured.

The Fool nodded, pressed both hands against his chest as a mark of respect and love, then left, following the path that Death had showed him. He wondered as he walked if the other souls had left willingly and what might be next upon their journey. Would they pass into the Underworld, or perhaps a heavenly realm? Would they meet again and, if so, what would be the next chapter in their story? Of course he would never really know because, as with all things in life, we cannot predict exactly what will befall us. We just have to be ready to embrace change, to die, and be reborn again in new ways. This was the cyclical nature of life, and the Fool finally understood what this meant.

As the darkness of night descended, he bowed his head low, found a place to rest, and said goodnight to the world.

The Death card closes a door in your life.
This may be an ending of sorts, but it is also
a new beginning.

14 TEMPERANCE

THEMES

Moderation

Peace

Balance

Purpose

THE FOOL LEFT THE FIELD BEHIND, and followed the rocky path, up and away toward the mountains. For the longest time he was alone with his thoughts, but that didn't matter to him. He had much to digest. It seemed like he'd been traveling for years, but he wasn't sure how many. He felt older in himself, not just from his experiences and the lessons learned, but in the way he moved. It was much harder to navigate rough terrain, and although some days he felt quite lively, he moved with less gusto. His muscles and limbs ached, and everything became more of an effort. That's not to say that he didn't enjoy it. He knew no other life than wandering from place to place, and it had given him great fulfillment. He had met many people, experienced different walks of life, and he felt enriched for it.

Life was good, and the Fool was content. When he was younger, to be happy was to be ecstatic, to feel an overwhelming pleasure and excitement, but he'd realized over time that this was a fleeting emotion. True joy came in those day-to-day moments when he felt satisfied and comfortable. As a youth the Fool craved adventure, and that was how his quest had begun. He had been full of optimism, ready to jump in and experience the thrill of the ride, but now he could see the value of simple pleasures like listening to early morning birdsong or the sight of a beautiful rose in bloom. Harmony and balance were more important than chasing an unobtainable dream. The Fool loved nothing better than to spend the day walking and meditating. He enjoyed engaging with his environment and connecting with nature. This gave him inner peace, and also a deeper understanding of how the world worked.

It was during a moment of deep reflection that the Fool became aware of a presence around him. His skin prickled, and the air felt charged with some otherworldly power. He looked to his left and right before gazing upward, and that's when he saw it descend between the clouds—an Angel, a glorious, winged being, with golden hair and a face that shone with grace.

The Fool held his breath; he couldn't quite believe that this was happening to him. He fell back upon the ground, shielding his eyes from the glare of the Angel's halo. As the light dimmed, he was able to see that it had one foot upon a rock, and one deep within a pool of water. It was as if it was balancing between two realms: that of water and the emotions; and also earth and all that is physical. Instantly the Fool understood the significance, and the importance of staying grounded, but also remaining "in the flow" of life. The symbol upon the Angel's robes caught his eye. It was a square encasing a triangle. The Fool knew from his studies that this represented humankind being bound by the laws of the Universe.

He watched silently as the Angel held two cups, one in each hand. Slowly, steadily, it poured water from one cup to the other, gently letting the liquid flow between the two in a continual cycle of give and take. The constant motion made him think of life and how there is an alchemy to the way everything moves, from the days and weeks to the seasons. He watched, mesmerized by this one action. It was as if it helped him focus his mind and see the world objectively.

The Angel didn't need to speak. The Fool could read every intention from the movement of the cups. He felt an aura of peace envelop him. His gaze softened, and he almost felt like he was drifting into a dream; and perhaps he was, for hovering low above the mountains he could see a golden crown. It was surrounded by bright light as it floated in mid-air.

What an astounding vision! thought the Fool. *But what does it signify?*

The Angel spoke then for the first time since appearing. Its velvety voice vibrated against the mountain range, issuing forth a distant echo.

"It represents the higher path that you and every human should take."

"But what does that mean?" asked the Fool again.

"It is a sign that you should stay true to your life's purpose and follow the path that you have been given."

The Fool nodded but wondered how anyone else might recognize their true purpose. He, after all, had been given the gift of the quest to discover his.

As if in answer, the Angel spoke again. "A person's true purpose is with them from birth. To find it, one must go within, and spend time in quiet contemplation. Let intuition guide the way, and most of all find a sense of balance and moderation in all things, for it is in the quieter times when we allow space into our lives that our true purpose emerges."

The Fool closed his eyes and absorbed the meaning of the Angel's wisdom. When he opened them again, the Angel had vanished and everything looked as it once had. The crown was gone, the skyline punctuated only by mountains.

A renewed sense of wellbeing washed over him. The Angel was right; quieter moments provided balance and moderation, an inner stillness that sharpened his perspective on the world, and also filled his life with harmony. This was the true meaning of Temperance—to seek out tranquility and find equilibrium in all things. The Fool had done this naturally during his journey, and the Angel had made him aware of it.

Yes, he was no longer the foolhardy, spirited young man who had stepped off a cliff at the start of the adventure, but the changes he'd experienced were necessary for his spirit to evolve. There was a time for everything, and the Fool recognized that stability, purpose, and peace were exactly what he needed, right now.

The Temperance card urges you to find
balance. Act in moderation and remain calm.
In stillness there is peace.

THE DEVIL.

15 THE DEVIL

THEMES

Enslavement

Shadow self

Restriction

Temptation

THE FOOL WAS ENJOYING THE NEXT STAGE of his journey. He had been uplifted by his visit from the Angel, and his mood was buoyant. He ambled onward, taking life at a leisurely pace. He had visited so many places and each one had left an imprint upon his heart. From abundant fruit-filled orchards to wild and magical woods, he'd walked the streets and roamed through fields and wasteland, climbed hills and mountains, and dipped to the lowest of valleys. He'd seen the ocean, walked along the coast, and dipped his feet into streams and rivers. There was so much beauty in the world around him, and he had drunk it all in like a thirsty man. Despite this, his soul had yet to be fully quenched, for the Fool had avoided one particular encounter. He knew it was coming, for he understood the natural order of things. For there to be light, there must also be shade, and within that there are dark, dangerous things that will rise to the surface. The Fool had witnessed Death, and learned the truth of its nature, but there were other things worth fearing; things that a person can only admit to themselves.

Now that he was in such a good place, it was time to address the darkness. He was strong enough to face any consequences that might unfold. The Fool settled down, and as night closed in around his shoulders, he lit a small fire. Breathing deeply, he let his gaze settle upon the flames.

He watched them tumble and thrash against each other. He saw them dance and flicker; slender fiery fingers reached out to him. He looked beyond the warmth, into the white-hot glare at the fire's center, and just when he could take the heat no longer, the Devil appeared.

Half man, half horned goat, the beast was a ghastly sight and the Fool recoiled in horror. He had not expected this, for while the Devil was demonic to look at, there was also something hypnotic about him. The Fool found it hard to tear his gaze away. He longed to look into the Devil's eyes, to feel the weight of that magnetic stare and yet he knew that if he did, he would be lost forever. As the image evolved, it seemed to solidify and the Fool could make out more details, like the inverted pentagram that hovered above the Devil's head, a symbol of the occult. The Fool shivered and tried to slither backward. Physically he did not want to be in the company of this wretched creature, but spiritually he felt he must stay. There was something to be gleaned from this experience; something that the Fool needed to acknowledge within.

The Devil watched, motionless; two giant black wings extended from his shoulders, wings from the vampire bat, an animal known for its ability to suck the blood from its prey. Was that what the Devil intended to do here? Would he ensnare the Fool, and bleed him dry, clawing every last bit of his soul from his body? It seemed a likely scenario, and yet the Fool felt like the Devil was hesitating. What was he waiting for?

At that moment, the beast began to rise from the ground and that's when the Fool saw that he had two victims chained to his podium. The naked man and woman did not speak or plead for help. They stood entranced, trapped within the Devil's grasp. Their faces were devoid of emotion; it was as if the life had been drained from them. As the Fool looked closer, he could see that the chains hung loosely around their necks, leaving a gaping space through which they could easily free themselves. Why didn't they? The Fool longed to ask, but then he noticed the small horns upon their heads, similar in style to the Devil's. Were they becoming like him? Perhaps being in his company had changed them.

Slowly, a wave of understanding passed over the Fool. The captives were victims of their own making. They had chosen this path, and it was up to them to free themselves, but they chose not to. How could this be?

Temptation. The answer came not in a word, but in a feeling; a desperate need that arose within the Fool's belly and crawled up his throat. The Devil was speaking to him, using the power of his emotions. These people had been drawn to this path, captured by their own needs and wants, and eventually enslaved by them. It could happen to anyone, the Fool realized. Small, simple things can become obsessions that take over, and pull you to the dark side.

He wondered then what his weakness was and what he needed to leave behind in order to become free. Was he trapped by ego, or some other negative trait? Perhaps he hadn't reached that stage yet, and it was more about acknowledging his darker impulses.

"A person is made of light and dark," came the voice in his head, and this time the feeling was gone, for this was the voice of reason.

"I am not the monster you think I am," the Devil said. "I exist, but I do not seek you out. It is you who seeks me."

The Fool had to agree. He had sought to converse with the Devil, to experience the light and dark at work within his soul. He was governed by desires and, at times, it had led him into danger. And while he couldn't say that he wouldn't be drawn by impulse again, at least now he was aware of it.

There was a moment of silence when it seemed like the air ceased to move. Then, as the breeze picked up once more and the fire flickered, the Devil was gone. He disappeared back into the flames and the ash, back into the Underworld from where he had come, taking his entourage and any sense of threat with him. The Fool felt relieved, for he had faced the darkness head on, and survived. He had addressed that side of himself and accepted its presence. He felt stronger because of it, and also weaker, for the same reason.

Taking a stick to poke the flames, he let the fire die down and cocooned himself in the warmth of his cloak. Softly, gently, he let slumber steal him away.

The Devil warns of temptation; you may be a slave to your desires or trapped in unhealthy patterns of behavior. Acknowledge this, and take the first step to freedom.

THE TOWER.

16 THE TOWER

THEMES

Chaos

Upheaval

Forced change

Revelation

The next day, the Fool gathered his belongings and continued on his way. Meeting the Devil had shaken him, but it had also made him whole in a way he didn't expect. He was aware of his shadow self, and able to see how it balanced the lighter aspects of his personality. He could harness the power within and draw the two together, in order to build a solid foundation. At least, that's what he thought, but there was still more to discover. During his journey the Fool had made many decisions, some built on knowledge and logic, some intuitive, and some to which he had given very little thought. The outcomes of all had been expected and he had learned much, but he was yet to encounter a life-changing event, something that would literally sweep the ground from under his feet.

He'd been climbing a rocky mountain for what seemed like days. It was a gentle incline at first, getting steeper toward the top, but the Fool was determined to reach the summit. He could see from some distance that there was a Tower there; built from stone bricks, it stood tall and proud and he longed to know what the view was like from the very tip. He imagined that it would be like flying; that he would feel as if he'd been suspended in mid-air, and he yearned for that excitement once more. As the Tower loomed above him, the Fool felt a shiver trickle down his spine. Was it fear of the unknown, or another emotion that he couldn't pinpoint? Whatever it was, he put it to the back of his mind. He had made it here at last, and he couldn't wait to reach the top. Lunging forward, he burst through the door and began to take the steps two at a time. He was in a race against time. The urge to see the kingdom from such a vantage point was overwhelming.

The staircase was spiral and tightly wound, and the Fool was running at such a pace that he soon began to feel dizzy. Everything around him was a blur. There were other people inside but they were in different rooms, some with windows, some without. The walls of the Tower began to constrict, or at least that's how it felt, like the bricks were pushing inward and the pressure was building. Despite this uncomfortable sensation the Fool would not be stopped. He had to reach the top, no matter what the cost, and so he persevered. Soon the peak was in sight; he could feel his legs trembling. His body felt heavy, as if the muscles had been replaced with stone. He licked his dry lips and tried to suck some moisture from the air. He gasped for breath and stuck his head out of the window. The view he'd been so desperate to see was blurry and he rubbed at his eyes.

What is happening here? he thought, but before his mind could offer some insight, there was an almighty bang, and the sky split in two. A flash of blinding light sliced through the air and hit the tip of the Tower. The building shuddered, as the lightning continued to bombard its structure. Beneath, the foundations shifted, and the Fool could feel the ground slipping from his feet. He screamed as the reality of the situation hit him. The Tower was collapsing, and there was nothing he could do to stop it. People were yelling, running, and leaping from windows. Flames surged through the main stairwell, and smoke billowed in every direction.

The Fool realized his fate was sealed. He had been so keen to reach the top that he had not considered how safe the tower was. His ego had been such that the only thing that mattered was his desire. Now he was paying the price. Even so, he could never have known this would happen. It came out of the blue. In one moment his life had turned upside down. The Fool looked around for something to hold on to, but there was nothing to steady him or break his fall. He could not avoid what was coming. All he could do was go with the flow, let the wave of destruction wash over him, and pray that he would emerge from the chaos stronger, more focused, and with a new lease of life.

Opening his arms wide, he let the force of a tremor lift him from his feet. Within seconds he was tumbling headfirst to the ground. As the Fool hit the earth, he landed with a squelch in a pool of mud.

It hurt a lot, but he was still in one piece, still able to breathe and put one foot in front of the other. He looked around him at the devastation. There was nothing left, just broken shards of stone, brick, and battered bodies, bruised, and limping away. He wondered then about the deeper meaning of the Tower. Like a fortress built on empty dreams and egotistical thoughts, it had become a prison to those who entered. A place that seemed to offer one thing, but it was all just for show. When the lightning struck, the Tower crumbled.

The lesson here was one of humility. To expect the unexpected, and to understand that life will test you. It was important to be open and humble, to learn what you could from the experience, so that you could be reborn. The Fool rose up onto his feet. He was beaten, his clothes in tatters, and his confidence too.

"Maybe this was just what I needed," he mused. "A shake up, a cataclysmic moment to force me to be real with myself. I do not know everything, and I never will."

He recognized then that the lightning bolt was not a weapon of mass destruction; it had illuminated the dark spaces, cast a light on what needed to change. Now it was up to him to take this knowledge and remold himself into a new shape. Staggering forward, shuffling a step at a time, the Fool began to find his balance. He could feel the ground beneath his feet once more and he was thankful for this gift.

The Tower card is a lightning bolt sent to shake things up. The ground may be shifting, but for every sudden change, there is enlightenment and growth.

17 THE STAR

THEMES

Hope

Faith

Divine blessings

Potential and renewal

THE FOOL WAS STILL SHAKEN by his fall from grace. The Tower was his ego, and now it was broken. He moved slowly, thinking about each step and what might be next upon his journey. Despite suffering a blow to his confidence, he felt somewhat free from earthly desires. His load had been lightened; he was able to reinvent himself, to look to the future with renewed hope. He walked on into the night, strolling through verdant meadows, gliding down slopes, and letting the land lead him on. His mind, now less troubled, felt bright and alert, and he gazed up at the blanket of stars that danced above him. It was an enchanting night and the air was sweet with the scent of honeysuckle. As he walked over yet another hilly mound, he saw that he was not alone. There, below him, was a woman. Her naked skin glistened in the moonlight; she seemed imbued with an inner glow, and he marveled at her beauty.

For a moment, he simply watched as she poured water from two separate vessels, nourishing the earth with a stream of liquid. He noticed that the water fell in five crystal-like rivulets, to represent the five senses from which he experienced the world around him. She had one foot in a pool of water, and one on dry land, and again the Fool knew this stance was synonymous with balance, for the water was her intuition, and the earth, the grounding, anchoring essence that held her in place. He breathed deeply, taking in the magical scene and he understood for the first time why it was so special. With his ego all but gone, he was able to witness things through fresh eyes. There was a purity in everything he experienced, an innocence that had been returned to him.

The woman seemed oblivious to his presence. Her focus was solely upon each tender action, her movements fluid. Even so, the Fool did not feel like an intruder. It felt right that he should be there, to witness everything. He noticed then the enormous star that seemed to rise in the sky behind her. Like a spotlight, it cast its luminescence over the scene, making her look even more radiant. The Fool wondered then if the woman herself might be made of stars, for there was something ethereal about her poise. It seemed to him that she was unsure of her human form and because of this everything she did was measured and graceful. She did not rush, because to her time meant nothing.

It was then that he noticed the seven accompanying stars that surrounded the bigger one. They framed the picture and offered their own light to the sky, each one equally important. They were tiny balls of fire wrapped up in a glistening form, like the seven chakras of the human aura. The meaning was clear—they were there to provide positive healing energy.

The Fool sighed. He felt privileged to be here in this moment, to see this angelic being and to understand her significance. He could not tear his eyes away from the central star; it seemed to be drawing him closer, and he longed to bathe in its glorious rays. The Fool found himself gliding down the slope toward the woman. He didn't need to move his legs; the light had lifted him from the ground, and he was floating. Exhilaration flooded every part of his being. The joy radiated from within his heart, and he knew that this was a sign that enlightenment was within his grasp. Pure loving energy flowed through him as he connected with the power of the Star, and he recognized that the divine spirit had always been in him. This realization filled him with hope. With the Star shining brightly, it seemed that the future was blessed. The Fool knew there would still be challenges ahead, things he could not determine or plan for, but his spiritual connection would always lift him up and help him to act with love.

It was then that the woman spoke into his mind. Her voice was clear and cloudless, like the sky above his head.

"Have faith, keep it in your heart, and you will always be blessed," she said.

The Fool smiled. "I will. I am reborn, and my hope is renewed. Thank you for sharing this divine gift with me."

"It has always been with you. It just takes a moment of peace and clarity to help you see this."

The Fool's heart hammered within his chest; he was excited for he could sense the potential in the air. Each day was a chance for a new beginning, the opportunity to transform any part of the future, and make the present more fulfilling. He laughed then, letting the happiness sweep over him. He spun around, his head turned to the stars, his arms wide open. If he could have embraced them, taken them into his soul, he would have done.

As the night gave way to the break of dawn, the Fool launched himself into a new day. He no longer felt fragile or broken from the events of the Tower; the Star had given him much to be thankful for. He had been reminded of his divine birth right, and his connection to the Universe. Standing tall, and drinking down the morning breeze, he looked around him. There was so much space, so much possibility. All he had to do was seize the moment, take a stride into the future and welcome it with open arms. The Fool grinned; there was nothing he loved more than a fresh start.

"Let the adventure of a new day begin!" he exclaimed and then, turning on his heel, he made that first step.

The Star is a beacon of hope and signals a positive period. There is light at the end of the tunnel, and joy is within your grasp.

THE MOON .

18 THE MOON

THE FOOL HAD BEEN IN A DREAM-LIKE TRANCE ever since his encounter with the Star. Its silvery rays had mesmerized him. They had permeated his soul. He floated down the hillside, through the next valley and up the hill with little effort. He was in a daze. He was lost in a flurry of daydreams and nothing else seemed to matter. The upbeat optimism that had first come to him in the Star's presence had been replaced by a hazy stupor. It was a light-headed sensation that had him tripping over himself, not paying much attention to anything. At first, he had felt a deep peace and a confidence that all would be well. Then over time, the joy had become almost euphoric. Had he taken it too far? Perhaps, but the Fool still had more lessons to learn.

As the wheel of time continued its motion, the Fool found himself wandering the landscape at night, which surprised him greatly for he had not seen the dark descend. He had not seen much of anything for a while. In truth he was lost, but in his bewildered state this meant nothing to him. He drifted onward, as the night's chill worked its way through his bones. He was aware of it, but not fully conscious. The Fool was in a halfway place, as if he had stepped through the veil and out of reality.

The Moon shone its glow from between two towers. Holding its place in the sky and casting a watchful eye on the ground below. It could see from this vantage point the Fool's journey, the winding path that now seemed to command his gait. It watched earnestly as the Fool staggered and tripped, one step forward, two steps back, making very little progress. So lost in dreamland was he, that he failed to notice the small pool up ahead. Stumbling forward, with a confusion of thoughts tumbling through his mind, he fell to his knees in the watery depths. The splash momentarily brought him back to his senses. The icy water made him gasp for breath.

"What is this? Where am I?" cried the Fool, as an anxious wind swept over him. Suddenly he felt very alone. He looked up and saw the Moon watching him. The dim rays of light that it cast upon the earth were not enough to illuminate the way ahead. They only revealed a small fragment of the view.

"Why can I not see where I am going?" said the Fool. He shook his head and rubbed at his eyes. "What is wrong with me?"

And then he remembered the thought processes that had led him to this point, the cacophony of ideas that swarmed his brain, some of them deep desires, some insane illusions, which had sprung from the depths of his subconscious. It was as if he'd been sleep walking. It was no wonder then that he ended up in such a strange place.

Shadows crept into the corners of his eyes; enormous beasts, flickering flames, and whispers of ghosts that tormented him.

"Go away!" he cried. "Leave me alone. I do not belong here. How did I get here?"

But he did not need to ask the question. He knew that this was his own doing.

The sounds of a wolf and dog howling and barking in unison cut through his thoughts, and he spotted them, standing across from the pool in a field of grass.

"How strange," he mused. "The wild and the tamed stand together, both making their voices heard."

It was true for him too—logic and reason were in a constant fight against the imaginary illusions in his head.

"How do I know what is real? How do I find the right path?"

It was then that he saw the lobster emerging from the water, a symbol of psychic power, breaking through the subconscious, and he understood that he too must let his intuition rise to the surface to see clearly. He gazed up at the face of the Moon and let the gentle light of illumination fill him up. It soothed his soul and calmed his whirling mind. Within the stillness, clarity stirred, and he realized that although the Moon triggered the imagination, it also instilled peace and understanding. Once more it seemed to the Fool that balance was at the heart of the matter: to know how far to go, to reach for inspiration without succumbing to the madness; to enjoy the fruits of your labors and feel elated, without letting it go to your head. The blessings of the Star were powerful and true, but there was work to be done. He must learn to cut through illusion, to let his mind wander, but not too far. The Fool realized he had been lost in the mire, but with the Moon's guiding influence he would find the right path. He could walk the road of daydreams, and still see the light of day.

"Mother Moon," he whispered, "let me harness the power of my imagination, let me experience those joyful highs, without losing myself completely."

The Moon seemed for a moment to smile. It was a beatific expression that encompassed happiness and serenity.

The Fool squinted in the darkness. He still could not see the road ahead fully, or where he was going, but with a little help and his intuition he might find his way back to civilization. The dog and the wolf had stopped making any noise. They regarded him warily from a distance, as if waiting for him to make a decision between the two.

"I do not choose either one of you above the other," said the Fool calmly. "I choose both of you, together. Let me be both wild and tamed in spirit."

Then, making his way around the pool, the Fool strode on toward the two towers. The Moon was sitting between them, and so it seemed that this was the direction he must travel in. He did not look too far ahead. Instead he gazed at his footsteps; he counted the beat of each one and the gentle rhythm of his breathing. He felt focused, like he was treading the invisible thread between the conscious and the unconscious mind.

The Moon suggests nothing is as it seems.
This is a time of illusion. Let your intuition guide
you and you will find illumination.

THE SUN.

19 THE SUN

THEMES

Delight

Joy

Warmth

Positive energy

Youthful exuberance

THE FOOL WATCHED THE DAWN OF A NEW DAY with interest. Like every day before, it was a new adventure, but today was special. After all he'd been through, the Fool felt truly grateful to watch the sunrise. He sat on the brow of a hill looking out across a vast expanse of land. He noticed the colors, the deep earthy browns, the soft spring greens and, in the distance, plateaus of corn yellow where the crops grew. He took those hues into his soul, and said "thank you," for this was his kingdom and the connection felt more potent than ever. He felt like he was seeing these things for the first time, looking through child-like eyes at his environment. Everything was tinged with wonder.

"How did I not notice this beauty before?" he asked, and in response he heard a blackbird sing. The uplifting melody filled his heart with joy, and he followed each note in his mind—listening and taking the song into his soul. The wind licked at his face. It caressed the curls of his hair and curved about his shoulders. It held him firmly in place, providing a cloak of inspiration from which he could peer at the world, and slowly let new ideas form in his mind.

"What a joy this is, to behold the day as it unfolds," he said triumphantly, for it was true, he felt victorious.

It had taken some time, but finally he understood the meaning of life and how each moment should be treasured.

He had felt the first stirrings of hope in his heart on meeting the Star, but his delight had turned to delusion, and confusion. It was easy to slip from one state of being to another, but being mindful was the key. To pay attention and be present allowed him to experience elation, to let his innate creativity flow, but also remain grounded.

The Fool gazed at the horizon, at the colors spilling forth upon the canvas of the sky. Soft pinks and ambers merged together to create a beautiful orange backdrop, as the golden orb of the Sun surged upwards. He squinted, letting the light of the Sun's rays filter through his aura until they were fully absorbed by his skin. He inhaled the radiance and took it into his soul.

"This is what happiness feels like," he announced and, standing up, threw his arms wide open as if to welcome the power of the Sun into his life. He imagined the orb to be a divine being, a god-like creature, whose rays of warmth could melt the hardest heart. In the distance it looked like a glittering jewel, a prize that no one could claim but everyone could share, for being in its presence was enough to raise a smile. It meant that all was well, and all would be well. With the Sun's dynamic energy on side, anything was possible.

It was then that the Fool noticed another presence by his side. He felt a gentle nuzzle to his shoulder and looked up to see a beautiful white horse standing next to him. It seemed that the creature was also watching and waiting for the Sun to take its place in the sky.

"Where did you come from?" the Fool asked, although he did not doubt that this glorious steed was meant for him.

"What a gift you are," he said as the horse whinnied softly.

He looked down then to the valley below. How inviting it looked.

"Do you feel like exploring?" he said, patting the horse upon the flank. The beast nodded its head and lowered a leg, so that the Fool could clamber on its back. "Then let us take advantage of this wonderful day!"

Together they rode at a steady trot, down the valley. There was no need to rush, not if they were to enjoy themselves fully. Instead, both horse and man looked with fresh eyes at their surroundings.

Finally they reached a high brick wall with a gate, which they passed through. On the other side they were met with the most magnificent sight—a row of majestic sunflowers, standing tall and proud, as if they had just lined up to greet their visitors. Their round golden faces were turned upward, following the path of the Sun as it journeyed through the sky. A symbol of strength and vibrant energy, the sunflowers held their position with such poise that the Fool couldn't help but smile.

In that moment, he felt so alive, as if he'd just been born; a tiny babe, new to the world, with not a care or worry. He was naked, free, and filled with vitality. The Fool opened his arms, and let the horse carry him forward. He had no need to fear, for he was safe, enveloped in loving energy that held him securely in place. He could be anything he wanted to be, do anything he wanted. This was his time to shine.

Above him the Sun watched, its expression beaming with delight. It grew in size and shape, as it bathed the land in warmth, and all the creatures big and small felt its closeness. The plants and flowers rose from their beds, stretching as high as they could to meet the Sun's glare, for they knew that this was the life-force that would help them blossom.

The Fool was also lost in the moment, but rather than staggering blindly down a path of dream and illusion, he was very much present and enthralled. He had finally recognized that he had the power to realize his dreams. He did not need to seek outside intervention, for it had always been within him.

"What an amazing day this is! I shall be sure to make the most of it!"

With that, he slid from the white steed and let the ground catch his fall. He pressed onward, his heart full to the brim with love, his head swimming in bliss.

The Sun brings warmth and happiness.
You are infused with vitality so step into the
spotlight—it's time to shine!

JUDGEMENT.

20 JUDGMENT

THEMES

Breakthrough

Absolution

Inner calling

Life's purpose

THE JOY OF THE SUN'S RADIANCE STAYED with the Fool for the longest time, fueling him with the energy he needed to continue his journey. It seemed that his quest would soon be coming to an end. The Fool could sense a shift in atmosphere, and he felt that time might be running out. This didn't worry him, for he knew in his heart that he was where he needed to be. He had learned much from his foray into the wilderness, and he had grown much too. His adventures had brought him into contact with all manner of beings. He had entered the spiritual realm, and felt his soul expand. He had learned of the importance of rules and guidance, and also how to trust his intuition. Now it was time for him to encounter his higher self, to be called into reckoning and to fulfill his destiny.

The Fool was aware that each and every soul made a promise before coming to Earth, an agreement upon their life's purpose. He too had committed himself to a cause, and now was the time to rise up and follow that path whole-heartedly, to choose which way to go, and what values he would take with him. His experiences would help him make the right decision, along with the wisdom that he gathered during his travels.

As the Fool passed through yet another town, he found himself walking toward a cemetery. It seemed fitting that he should be in such a spiritual place at this moment in his life. He stopped for a moment to ponder those who lay beneath the ground. What had brought them here? How had they met their end? If in fact it was the end, for the Fool had learned from Death that endings were new beginnings in disguise. He wondered about the kind of people they had been, and if their experiences had been similar to his own. Perhaps everyone had their own spiritual quest to challenge them before they could move on to the next phase. Silently and solemnly he said a prayer in his head. He prayed for their salvation, and for those they had left behind. He prayed too for himself, for he knew that he would also have to take this next step at some point in the future.

Just as he was about to leave, he felt the heavens open. There was a dramatic clap of thunder as the sky split in two. The Fool staggered backward, shielding his eyes from the blinding light.

Gradually the brightness dimmed, and he saw a giant Angel emerge. It was the Angel Gabriel, with enormous red wings and a trumpet pressed to his mouth. He looked down upon the Earth, at the graves that lay before him, and he blew into the bugle. A loud ringing sound issued forth. It echoed through the mountains in the distance. It resonated deep within the Fool's soul. The trumpet of truth called to him, awakening some part that had lain dormant. At the same time, the souls of the dead emerged from their earthly graves. They burst through the soil, their arms outstretched. They reached up to the heavens, to the Angel in the sky, and cried for their salvation. Resurrection had come, and they were reborn.

The Fool gasped; he had never seen such a spectacle. Those who had once been dead were called to arms, to rise and feel the warmth of the sun upon their faces. He, too, felt the calling, but in a different way. For him, it was about accepting his true purpose. It was time to take the ultimate step, the one that would bring him back to Earth. In one respect, it would be the end of his adventure, but it would also be the beginning of a new one.

The Fool closed his eyes and placed his hands upon his heart. He listened intently to his intuition, and let his spirit speak to him. Yes, he knew what he must do, what had always been intended for him. It was time to take all of those teachings and put them into practice, to share his knowledge with the rest of the world.

He watched the gathered moving forward, pulling themselves from the depths of the earth. How hard it must be to extricate themselves from that which had held them tightly for so long, but isn't that what new beginnings are all about?

Being summoned, and making a breakthrough, was never easy but always rewarding. The Fool let those thoughts settle in his mind.

He, too, was ready to make that breakthrough, even if it meant leaving his quest behind.

The Angel Gabriel had now vanished and only the clouds remained. They circled above the Fool's head, but they did not cloud his mind. He was clear on what was needed. It was time to step up spiritually and make his mark. Turning from the cemetery, the Fool could see the mountain range ahead, but unlike many of the others that he had passed through, this one was different. It represented the obstacles and judgments that lay ahead. He was very much aware that his chosen path would be tricky, that returning to the life he had known would be fraught with challenges, but the Fool was ready.

Taking a deep breath, which he drew from the soles of his feet up into his chest and lungs, the Fool stepped out for what would be the last time upon his journey. He would conquer the mountains; he would reach the other side, and he would share all of the lessons he had learned so that others might navigate their own spiritual quest. This was his calling, the true purpose that his higher self had revealed to him. At last he felt absolved and ready to be the person he was meant to be!

The Judgment card calls you to rise up.
You are about to make some kind of breakthrough.
Let go of the past, and step into the future.

THE WORLD.

21 THE WORLD

THEMES

Wholeness

Completion of a cycle

Integration

Accomplishment

Finally, the Fool emerged at the top of the mountain range, and there before him was a very different landscape, but one he knew well. It was his home. It was just a heartbeat away, another leap of faith, but he could see it clearly as the clouds parted. It was some miles in the distance, and a long way down, but that did not bother the Fool. He had come so far and was ready to return, to finish the cycle. The circle was complete, and he was back at the same point, but he was a very different person to the one who had set out all that time ago. His travels had brought him spiritual sustenance, a renewed sense of self, and a confidence that he could never have imagined. It had been arduous, and he had worked hard to reach this point. Now it was time to reap the rewards, to stand and have his moment in the sun. He wondered how others would see him—would they notice the change? He felt it was obvious, and that he had grown both physically and emotionally.

He looked then at the space directly in front of him and noticed that the atmosphere had changed. A blurry, shimmering shape had materialized in the form of a woman. She hovered within a circular wreath that hung in the air. To most this would have appeared strange, but the Fool was not startled. He had witnessed so much during his quest that this seemed quite normal. The woman was draped in purple cloth and was dancing. Her head was looking backward, her body facing forward, which the Fool thought was apt. She honored her past, but was ready to step into her future, and he felt the same way. He recognized the importance of what had gone before, the effort he had put in, but he also wanted to move forward.

In her hands she held two wands similar to those used by the Magician, who the Fool had met right at the beginning of his quest. Again, this seemed appropriate and symbolic of the completion of his journey.

Everything is cyclical, thought the Fool, and he noted the wreath also represented the circular nature of life. The woman simply needed to step through to the other side, to move on to the next phase.

Around the wreath four figures hovered; a lion, a bull, a cherub, and an eagle. Each one was a guide to the process of change, and the four fixed signs of the Zodiac. The Fool realized he had seen them before. They were present during his vision of the Wheel of Fortune.

"Everything is connected," he whispered.

The vision was breathtaking, and the Fool gazed in wonder. He could see that the four fixed signs represented the four elements of earth, air, fire, and water, and that they were also the four seasons, and the corners of the World.

"The World," he said, for he finally understood what this image was all about. It was a symbol of fulfillment and completion, a moment to acknowledge success, and to revel in the joy of doing and being. Like the World, he was whole. His task was complete. He could enjoy this time and reflect upon his journey. Indeed, he felt that it was important to evaluate everything and consider how far he had come. The highs and lows, the trials and tribulations, they were all a part of the past but still significant. Like the woman before him, he could honor both what had gone, and what was to come. He could use the knowledge and life lessons he'd gained to help him in this new phase.

The Fool felt excited once more but, unlike his younger self stepping out into the world for the first time, this excitement was colored with experience. He knew there would be ups and downs. Nothing was ever straightforward in life, but that was the joy of the journey.

For a moment he held the gaze of the woman within the wreath. He watched her dance, and he felt himself moving too, swaying to a distant melody.

This is what it is like to be in the flow, in sync with the Universe and your life's purpose, he thought.

Eventually, the wavering shape of the woman faded from view. All that was left was the wreath, hanging aloft. The circular shape beckoned him closer, and the Fool shuffled toward the edge of the cliff. He didn't look down, or up, he just stared straight ahead.

"Out there is my future, my destiny, and I must fulfill it." He spoke with confidence. "I will share my knowledge with the rest of the world. I will show them using the colorful images and visions that I have witnessed how to navigate a path and work with fate. Each picture will have a purpose, a meaning that they will be able to read, just by looking at it. They will understand which stage of my journey it represents, and they will be able to apply it to their own life. In doing this, they will have a blueprint to which they can work. That is my calling. That is what I am meant to do. I will share my story with everyone in the hope that they, too, can take it to their hearts."

The Fool pledged his worth and then, just as he had done at the beginning of this tale, he took a step—off the mountain and into the ether.

He passed through the wreath and out the other side, re-entering the World whole and refreshed. His sense of self was restored and his spiritual essence intact. At last he knew his life purpose and was aware of his place. It was the end of one cycle, and the beginning of something new.

His quest had been a success.

All was as it should be.

The Fool's journey was finally complete.

The World card signals success; you have reached your goal so take a moment to enjoy this feeling. A cycle is complete, and fulfillment is yours.

ACE of PENTACLES.

ACE of SWORDS.

ACE of CUPS.

ACE of WANDS.

The Minor Arcana

Like a regular pack of cards, the Tarot contains four numbered suits (pentacles, swords, cups, and wands) and court cards (Page, Knight, Queen, and King), and each suit represents a theme throughout. It is easy to misjudge these cards and consider them less important than the weightier Major Arcana, but they're integral to the pack and play a key role in deciphering your reading. They deal with issues that arise in your daily life, and are things we can all identify with—the highs and lows, the heartaches, and the joys are all played out here. It is no wonder then that these cards resonate so powerfully.

Each suit has its place within the pack, offering insight and a perspective on a different facet of life. With the suit of pentacles, the core needs of security and abundance arise. We see the role that money plays, and how it can change us. We bear witness to the riches of life, and how we can enjoy prosperity and make it work for us. In the suit of swords, we learn about passion—what drives us forward to achieve, and those emotions, base or otherwise, that make us act in different ways. The suit of cups might be considered the gentler suit, as it deals with affairs of the heart, but do not underestimate the quest for love and the challenges and blessings that it brings. Finally we are cast into the realm of ideas, with the suit of wands. Where does inspiration come from, and how can we tap into this energy to create the things we want? We venture forth into the world of the imagination and discover the role communication plays in our relationships and the opportunities that come our way.

The stories in this section will help you form a deeper understanding of what each card means, and its place within the suit. By following the overall narrative, you'll go on a journey and make a personal connection with the themes therein. Each card offers a different interpretation, but it is only a small piece of the puzzle and a snapshot of how your life might unfold. The choices you make every day manifest your future, and the Minor Arcana is the perfect tool to help you navigate a path to fulfillment.

The Suit of Pentacles

ACE OF PENTACLES

IN A LAND BETWEEN TIME AND SPACE, where magic is a whisper upon the breeze, there lived three sisters. Each one had flowing hair that shone all the colors of the rainbow in the morning sun. As beautiful as they were, they were seeking their place in the world and, having little wealth, they made a simple life working the land within their community. Every day was the same hard toil, and while each girl gave her best, their intentions differed.

The eldest, Penny, secretly resented the life to which she was bound. She dreamed of traveling farther afield, of spreading her wings in the finest of gowns, and feasting daily from a bejeweled throne. The middle girl, Celine, just wanted to keep everything for herself. She believed she worked the hardest and deserved the lion's share, which she would gather to her skirts and keep close to her heart.

Then there was Charity, the youngest, and some might say sweetest, of the three. She enjoyed her work and felt truly blessed to have two such wonderful sisters and a role to play in her village. They lived and they worked, and life was unremarkable, up to a point.

But as with all things, change must come, and it would touch their world in the most unusual way. The sisters were to be given the gift of abundance, and it came from out of the blue as these things often do. On journeying home from the field, they took a detour through the woods to pick some flowers, and that's where they found their bequest hidden amongst the deep grasses, at the base of the old oak tree. They would have missed it too, if it hadn't been for a spiral of sunlight that snaked through the branches to reveal a glint of gold so bright, they had to shield their eyes.

"How beautiful!" Charity cried, as she pulled the prize from the earth; a single, yet enormous piece of gold shaped like a giant coin. "It must have fallen from the heavens."

"Oh my!" yelled Penny, tearing it from her sister's fingers. "Look how it shines!"

"We must hide it," whispered Celine, clawing it away from Penny and pressing it safely into her chest.

"But it doesn't belong to us," said Charity. "Someone may have lost it."

"It's ours!" said Penny and Celine together.

The three sisters looked at each other, and in that moment they realized they had been given a gift, a bountiful blessing bestowed upon them from the Universe. What they did with this rich offering could change their fate, and the way they viewed the world forever.

TWO OF PENTACLES

THEMES

Balance

Juggling

Harmony

Decisions

A CHILL BREEZE WHISTLED THROUGH the swarthy branches of the oak, canceling out the sunshine, and bringing a gray shadow to the heart of the woods where the sisters were gathered.

"Perhaps we should put it back," Charity suggested, nodding to the golden prize within Celine's tight grip, but her sisters were having none of it. Instead they were playing a game of catch, as each one desperately tried to snare the coin for themselves.

"It's mine, it's mine!" they cried in unison, while pushing and pulling in a see-saw motion.

"It is surely big enough for you both to have a piece?" said Charity.

"But who decides how to share?" asked Penny. "We must strive for balance between us all, we must be fair!"

There was a moment of silence, and then a rustling sound from overhead. The canopy of the giant oak was moving, trembling, as the branches parted to reveal a curious-looking character. Not unlike a pixie, he was dressed in a tunic and a pointy hat. He landed lightly at their feet and in one fluid movement and a lavish swirl, clicked his fingers twice. Within seconds the gold coin split in two, one piece in each of his hands.

"'Tis a simple game of balance and harmony," he said, looking at their bemused faces. "There is no need to panic, fair ladies. You simply need to manage your time and work out what is most important. The gift of abundance will do the rest."

The little man then began to dance, hopping from foot to foot, while letting the coins swing high and low. The sisters watched, open-mouthed. What kind of magic was this? They had never seen such a thing before and were transfixed.

It was Charity who eventually found her voice and spoke.

"Kind sir, thank you for your mystical intervention. We are most grateful for your pearls of wisdom. We will take this to heart, and remember to juggle, and find the balance in our financial affairs."

She smiled as the small man placed a coin in each of her hands.

"An important lesson has been learned this day," he said. "Be sure to recall it when the time comes."

With that, he executed a graceful pirouette and was gone, leaving only a flurry of dust in his wake.

The girls looked up expecting to see his cheerful face peering down from the crown of the tree, but if he was there, he was well hidden and as silent as a mouse.

THREE OF PENTACLES

THEMES

Collaboration

Teamwork

Harmony

Industry

THE SISTERS FOLLOWED THE WINDING PATH through the woods, each one lost in their own thoughts. There was so much to consider, from the bounty in their hands, to the magical man and his sage words. The sound of their footfall became a gentle pattern, a rhythm that they made together, tap, tap, tap. The sharp, shrill birdsong overhead was the only accompaniment, as they focused their attention on moving forward.

It was Charity who eventually noticed that they had gone off the trail.

"How strange!" she said, taking in the unfamiliar surroundings. They had somehow made their way to a clearing, a circular space with a small brick building and an arched window.

"I have never seen this before."

"It looks like it was once a chapel," remarked Penny, "but look at it, it's almost falling down!"

"It needs rebuilding," Celine sniffed, "but there's nothing we can do."

"I think there is," said Charity. She was already making her way toward the crumbling window arch. Quickly, as she had seen the little man do, she clicked her fingers three times, and the coins tripled in her hands.

"How did you do that?" Penny gasped. "It must be magic gold."

Charity ignored her, and gently she lifted a coin into a gaping hole, bridging the gap and helping to keep the structure firm.

"If we work together, we can make it strong again."

Celine shrugged. "But then we'll have to part with our coins."

"Only for a short while, until we find something else that will do the job," said Charity.

Her sisters reluctantly agreed, and positioned a coin in place, building a secure frame for the window to sit neatly. They used the tools from their field work to chisel and position each one, and chipped away at some of the discarded stones, making them the perfect size to slot in place. They worked in harmony, humming along with the breeze—and while it took some time, it felt like no time at all because they were united in their mission.

Eventually they stopped and surveyed their handiwork. The stone chapel seemed to take on a new light, as if their efforts had somehow restored its sense of purpose. The window frame was secure, and the coins were replaced by perfectly crafted lumps of stone.

"Amazing!" they cried together.

At that point, a gentleman dressed in ceremonial garb joined them. The girls were quite surprised at the entrance of the stranger, but he insisted he had been there a while watching them work.

"I didn't wish to disturb you, you looked so harmonious," he beamed. "And you fixed my little chapel, for which I am deeply grateful."

The girls laughed and clapped their hands.

"See what we can do when we work together," Charity said, smiling.

Her sisters nodded and they linked arms. Their bond renewed and their moods lifted, they began to retrace their steps and make their way home, each with a large gold coin in their pocket.

FOUR OF PENTACLES

THEMES

Need

Greed

Control

Security

AFTER WALKING SOME MILES, the sisters reached the brow of a hill where they could clearly see the outskirts of their small town in the distance. They had come far and made a great detour through the wood and out the other side. They had learned much from their curious journey and pondered their hopes and dreams. Now that they had been blessed with wealth, anything was possible. They had the power and potential to create their perfect life, but what was that exactly? Each sister had a different view.

They stopped for a moment at the stone throne to catch their breath and take in the outline of buildings upon the horizon. The throne itself was colossal, a relic from a different age. A symbol of prosperity, it was thought that an ancient King had built it so that he could survey his kingdom. From here, he could look down and see everything that belonged to him and how much he was worth. Suddenly as if inspired by some unseen force, Celine grabbed the coins from her sisters and scrambled up on the throne.

"See how it fits me," she said proudly. "I am as wealthy as a Queen!"

She grasped at the coins, desperately trying to hold them in her arms.

"They're all mine," she whispered, and her eyes flickered with greed.

"They're ours," said Penny, walking toward her.

"Don't come any closer," said Celine. "They're mine, I'll look after them and keep them safe." She was trying to balance a coin upon her head, while clinging on to the other two.

"They're not yours. You didn't earn them. They're a gift, and something we can share, not just amongst ourselves," said Charity gently. "Think of the good we can do."

Celine grimaced as if she'd been physically punched. Her fear of losing what she held in her arms made her feel uncomfortable. She was already struggling to juggle the three coins, but then something happened that made it even more impossible.

Charity clicked her fingers again, and the three became four, two of which tumbled to the floor.

Celine gasped and stretched out her feet, planting them firmly on each coin.

"They won't get away from me!" urged Celine. "I deserve to be rich."

"I'm sorry," said Charity. "You can't keep them all to yourself. It won't do you any good."

For a moment it seemed like time stood still. Each sister was rooted to the spot. Celine sat stony-faced, afraid to make the slightest movement, in case the coin from her head should topple and the ones at her feet should follow suit.

"I will not lose everything," she hissed.

"Sometimes you have to lose, to win," replied Charity.

FIVE OF PENTACLES

THEMES

Loss

Isolation

Poverty

Worry

T HE SKY DARKENED AND A GUST OF WIND came from nowhere, multiplying the coins once more and adding an extra one to the bounty. The sharp breeze whipped against the throne, battering the rough stone. Tendrils of air slashed at Celine's fingers and curled beneath their grip. The coin on her head was the first to fall, and then the one nestled close to her heart. The wind continued its onslaught, lashing at her skirts, knocking her backward. Her feet rose into the air and the coins beneath were gone.

She watched in horror as they rolled down the hill toward the town. There was nothing she could do; no way to prevent their escape. They were tumbling at such a speed to who knows where. Celine wailed.

"Why? Why could I not keep them?"

"Because you clung on too tight," said Charity.

"But now I have nothing, I've lost everything!"

Charity placed a hand on her sister's shoulder. "All will be well; we have had nothing before."

Celine clasped her head in her hands. She had never felt so alone, so isolated from everything. If only she could have held on tighter, but there was nothing to be done. She had let the gift slip from her fingers and now they would all suffer.

She raised her head to the sky and said a silent prayer. *I'd give anything to have them back,* she thought, but the heavens were not in a generous mood. Instead, the darkness turned to a blanket of white; thick and heavy, it seemed to press down on her. The icy air seeped into her skin until the chill reached her heart. She could hardly breathe and wondered if she too had turned to stone like the throne she sat upon, but then she felt hands reaching for her, whispers of skin touching hers. She looked up to see a small wounded man, gazing at her.

"The snow is coming," he whispered.

Celine gasped. "Where did you come from?"

"I am but a ghost who wanders this place, a memory of what has been lost and a reminder to those souls who need it on days such as this, that life is more precious than any treasure."

Celine shook her head and rubbed at her eyes. "This is not real."

"I am as real as your desires," he said sadly, each part of him fading from her sight. She reached for him and stumbled forward, but her sisters were there to catch her.

"The snow is coming," they yelled. "We have to go before it sets in."

Celine nodded blindly and let them lead her down from the lofty stone perch. Together they stumbled from the brow of the hill, their feet sliding on the damp grass. The snow was coming fast, great swathes like sheets that flapped and then finally settled on the ground. What was once vibrant green had now turned white. All the colors had drained away and been replaced by a blank canvas. From here it was hard to imagine what had come before. The landscape was transformed, but it wasn't the only thing. Celine too felt a change within. Her cold heart was thawing. The wounded man had helped her to realize the error of her ways. Her neediness had created fear, and this had destroyed everything. If she wasn't careful, she would end up like him, a lost soul wandering aimlessly, searching for something that no longer mattered. If she had been more open and sharing, let the others hold their coins, then all would be well. Instead she had tried to control them through greed, and it had ended badly. She pulled her cloak around her and began the descent toward home.

SIX OF PENTACLES

IT WASN'T LONG BEFORE THE SISTERS made it to the main road leading to market. It was a widely traveled thoroughfare, a route made by traders, farmers, and those who were simply passing through. Today it was quiet, and as the snowy weather cleared and the sun began to shine once more, clumps of grass and flowers emerged. With damp-sodden skirts and cloaks that lay heavy upon their shoulders, there seemed little to smile about, but Charity, forever hopeful, tried to look on the bright side.

"We have each other, and we are almost home. All is not lost."

"But we don't have the magical coins," whined Penny.

Celine remained stoic in her silence. Deep in thought she was pondering the error of her ways and fixed her stare on the ground as she walked. So lost in her own thoughts was she that she failed to see the man sitting at the side of the road and nearly stumbled over him.

"Oh, I'm so sorry," she said and, looking at his somber face, added, "You look lost, is there anything I can do?"

The man rose from his spot and offered a hand.

"It is I who should ask you that question. You are soaked to the skin."

It was obvious from his fine outfit and velvet cloak that this was no peasant.

"I am fine," smiled Celine weakly. "These are my two sisters, and we are on our way home."

"Then perhaps I can walk with you some of the way, or at least offer my assistance."

As they continued to move slowly toward the town, two more weary travelers in thread-worn garments joined them. They too seemed in need, like the sisters. As they walked the man regaled them with a strange tale of magical coins raining down from the heavens.

"It was quite odd the way they suddenly appeared, rolling down from the hillside." He opened his arms wide. "I have no need for more money. I have more than enough and so when you found me, I was pondering my situation and what to do with this bountiful gift, and I have decided to give it to all of you."

With that he dug into his pockets and scattered the coins to the gathered group, including the girls and the two men who had joined them. The sisters were dumbfounded. Their gift had been returned to them when they least expected it.

"I am sure you will use it wisely," said the man. "Remember the importance of giving and receiving."

"Thank you!" the girls cried, as the stranger said farewell and strode ahead.

"What luck!" laughed Penny.

"What kindness," sighed Charity.

Celine simply smiled; she finally understood an important truth—at the heart of sharing, there is true joy and wealth. It was a lesson she would not forget in a hurry.

SEVEN OF PENTACLES

THEMES

Investment

Planning

Perseverance

Growth

THE WALLED GARDENS AND COURTYARDS of the town were a glorious sight as the sisters got closer to home. A symbol of wealth and prosperity, they hinted at the luxury that might be hidden within. It was something Penny had always wondered about. She longed to live in a grand townhouse, with servants aplenty. It wasn't that she wanted to be waited on hand and foot; to her the joy was in "having" for a change. Their humble lifestyle meant no finery, no treats or beautiful objects. Everything was plain and simple and Penny had grown to hate that, but at least she now had the chance to experience some of these things. She gripped the golden pennies in her pocket and smiled.

Their journey home would take them through the town and out the other side, where the poorer villagers lived. Here there were only fields and crops, clumps of greenery, and a few trees. A young man was busy tending to his crop. He stopped for a moment and waved to the sisters.

"If only it would grow faster," he sighed, pointing to a shrub. "I need to sell my wares."

"It's a pity we can't grow money," said Penny.

"Perhaps we can!" said Celine suddenly. "We've learned that if we give back, and we work together and put in the effort, then we'll be rewarded, right?"

Charity shrugged. "These are magical coins, after all; I believe we can do anything we want with them!"

"What are you talking about?" asked Penny, frantically looking from sister to sister.

"If we work together, we can grow wealth gradually, sow the seeds and invest in the town's future," said Celine, and with that she grabbed the man's hoe and made a trough in the ground near the shrub. Within seconds she'd pressed her coins into the soil, and with the help of Charity, who also offered up her treasure, they were covering them over. They patted down the ground, and watered it well, then made a wish for abundance.

"Are you mad?" yelled Penny. "Money doesn't grow on trees!"

"But it does grow if you work for it," said Charity, "and these coins are magic, remember?"

"Well I'm not giving mine to the earth. I want to enjoy my wealth now."

Penny stuck her head in the air and began to walk at speed back toward the town. Her mind was made up; she would treat herself today and make the most of her sudden good fortune. She had no time for saving or building a future when she could experience true pleasure now.

Her sisters watched her go, and then returned their attention to the newly planted coins of wealth, which had already started to sprout through the soil.

EIGHT OF PENTACLES

For the next few days, Charity and Celine worked hard trying to nurture and cultivate the money tree that they hoped would grow for their village. They knew little about magical plants, but they were prepared to learn and practice the techniques. Taking instruction from the farmer's hand, and watching what he did as he tended to each sapling and seedling, they soon became skilled. To some, it might have seemed a tedious task, repeating the same things every day to ensure their little shrub survived. To the sisters it was essential, and they delighted in the small and steady changes that they saw.

While Penny hunted down the treasures of the town and adorned herself in finery, her sisters chose to work quietly and steadfastly. Their focus never wavered, for they had a mission in mind.

"You are doing so well," the farmer's hand said. "You have been the ideal apprentices. You have watched and learned, and then practiced. Now you are seeing the results."

He pointed to the tiny saplings that were bursting from the ground and seemed to reach for the stars. Slowly the vines had spread, and were now snaking a path up the nearest tree.

"How is that possible?" he asked.

"It's magic," said the girls in unison, and indeed it was, for the coins had begun to grow along the length of the trunk and were thriving.

As each coin grew in size, it seemed to bloom like a flower and cast a golden glow over the earth. When it reached its fullest, it would fall to the ground where the farmer's hand would catch it, and carve a pentacle pattern into its face as a way to identify it. Soon the pile of coins had grown, and there were eight pieces of gold, like jewels stacked in a row.

"That is quite an accomplishment," said the young man. "What will you do with your newly grown riches?"

The sisters looked at each other. It was a good question, and they hadn't discussed it openly, but each one knew in their heart what the other would say, in that moment.

"We will share it, of course."

The young man looked puzzled. "Don't you want to hold on to your wealth?"

Charity grinned. "Oh you misunderstand me Sir, we are still wealthy, but the riches we value are a different kind of treasure. This," she said, pointing to the coins, "is a gift that we want everyone to enjoy."

NINE OF PENTACLES

THEMES

Luxury

Abundance

Independence

Pleasure

WHILE THE TWO SISTERS CONTINUED TO WORK HARD in the fields outside their home, Penny also plowed ahead. Being independent in heart and mind, she had a plan for her wealth; she wanted to enjoy it, and this she did with gusto. While some might say she was frivolous, Penny was determined to make the most of her prize—after all, she'd been blessed with a gift.

She swapped her dowdy skirts for satin gowns and velvet outer coats and cloaks, looking every part the wealthy maiden. She found a house within the town walls with a beautiful courtyard and an even more abundant garden. It was a glorious flower-filled space, and the perfect haven for a woman of substance. She imported fruit trees and exotic singing birds to keep her company while her sisters toiled, and she would stand and tell tales to the birds.

She would speak of her exploits, and how she had reached this pinnacle in her life. Some might say she was gloating, but in fact Penny knew how precious the gift of abundance was, and so she made every day count. She missed her sisters and the life they had together, but she didn't want to waste a moment of her fortune. In truth, she enjoyed life, but there was something missing, something that all the money in the world couldn't buy her.

Whenever she walked through the town, she would hear people whisper, "Oh how gorgeous is that dress, how very wealthy that woman must be!"

It made her heart flutter with pride, and she wished she had someone to share her joy with, but instead of feeling sad she would return to her garden. Being in nature and feeding the birds helped her feel like she had a place in the world.

One morning, as she was dressed in her finest gown with a bird upon her arm, she heard the sound of laughter carried on the breeze. It was the sweetest music to her ears, and it made her heart sing, for she recognized the voices and knew in an instant that this was the treasure she missed the most. Yes, life was good, and she had every right to enjoy it, but there were different kinds of wealth, which could not be measured in gold coins. Family, friendship, love, and laughter; these were the purest gifts and the things she really needed to make each day count.

TEN OF PENTACLES

THEMES

Wealth

Success

Happiness

Gratitude

Penny closed her eyes and listened for the happy melody that had caught her attention. It had been fleeting, a trickle of sound upon a gentle breeze, and yet it had awoken something within her. She focused on the rise and fall of her chest and the sound of her own breath, and when she felt totally relaxed she let her attention wander beyond the garden walls. Her awareness extended outward and she sensed not only what was audible, but also the emotions in the laughter. She called upon her sisterly bond and let that pull her toward the tune.

Soon, and without even realizing it, Penny passed through the town gates, and was making her way to the family home. Her feet barely touched the ground. She felt as light as a feather, as if her need to be with those she loved was carrying her through the air. When she finally reached the field beyond the small cottage, her sisters were waiting for her.

"We knew you were coming," smiled Charity.

"We felt it, in here," said Celine, tapping her chest.

Penny gasped as she surveyed what had once been their home and took in the small audience waiting for her. The crumbling walls had been rebuilt, and the smallholding for the animals restored to its full glory. The garden, which had always been more of a yard, was as glorious as her own and heaped with flowers and fruits. Her sisters too looked different, not only in the fine clothes they wore, but in the color of their cheeks and their sparkling eyes. There was a vitality there that Penny had never seen before. A crowd of neighbors had gathered, and they were clapping and cheering. Children and dogs played between the feet of the adults, and there was so much laughter. Everyone was happy, vibrant, and alive.

"What happened here?" asked Penny.

"The gift of abundance," said Charity. "We decided to share it, to work together in the community, and create even more, so that no one is left out. We put our magical coins to work and, in taking the time to nurture them, they have grown and our wealth has multiplied."

Penny smiled. "You have so much more than that—you have family riches, happiness, and love—things that have true meaning."

"And so do you!" cried her sisters, as they embraced her in their arms. "Today is a day of celebration, so let us be thankful for all the wonderful blessings in our lives." And with that they linked arms and danced with joy in their hearts.

PAGE of PENTACLES

PAGE OF PENTACLES

THE SISTERS WERE HAPPY TO BE BACK together again. Everything was as it should be. They were a team once more, and able to share their joy and talents. The magical coin that they had found in the woods had proved to be their making, but it hadn't been an easy journey. Along the way they had learned the true value of wealth, how it could transform thoughts and feelings, and influence actions. From hoarding, and grasping at the pennies, to using riches for status, the sisters now realized that money was a good thing, if you learned to work with it and share it with the wider community.

The gold coins had multiplied and bore fruit, and the money tree they had so carefully cultivated was thriving. This in turn meant that all of the villagers benefited from the bounty. They were able to clothe and feed their neighbors, help to renovate their homes, and make them safe and joyful places to be. The townsfolk were at first amused by this new development, but soon realized that the villagers were making a profit, and that the changes were permanent. No longer was there a divide between the poor and the rich, those who struggled to survive from day to day, and those who lived in the lap of luxury. All things and all people were equal. This may have bothered some at first, but in time they realized it was a good thing. They could live in harmony, without fear or worry. Need was a word that had lost its meaning.

And so it was that on one perfect morning in the spring, as the flowers bloomed in the fields and the grass was damp with dew, an emissary from the King's court appeared. He was a young Page dressed in a tunic as green as the meadow he stood upon.

"Tell me, what is happening here?" he asked the sisters. "How did you create such wealth and unity when you had nothing?"

The girls smiled and said, "Let us show you."

Handing the Page a gold coin, they told their story of the journey they had made to reach this point. They told him of the magical gift, what they had learned, and also how they had planted the tree to help everyone.

"And could anyone do this?" asked the Page.

"Anyone with an open heart, who wants to welcome the flow of abundance into their life," said Charity. "To manifest great wealth, you must be prepared to work, to give thanks for what you receive, and share the love."

The Page was full of excitement and motivation at the thought of being able to create such a vibrant future for everyone. He left full of ideas and with a smile upon his face.

KNIGHT of PENTACLES.

KNIGHT OF PENTACLES

THEMES

Hard work

Productivity

A practical and honest man

I T WAS ONLY A FEW DAYS AFTER THE ARRIVAL of the Page that another visitor came to the village with a quest in mind. Dressed in silver armor and riding a dark horse, he was a man on a mission, a Knight, who was also a royal Prince, and his purpose was to gather knowledge. As he moved closer to the meadow where the sisters lived, they could see that he carried a gold coin in his hands: the same gold coin they had given to the Page. Slowly, his horse came to a standstill in front of the girls. In one fluid movement, he found his feet on the ground and bowed low.

"Ladies," he said. "It is an honor to meet you. I have heard much about your success, and the work you have done for your village. My Page is full of enthusiasm for your efforts and informs me that you know how to make money grow on trees."

The sisters laughed, but it was Charity who spoke for them.

"There is more to it than that, but if you are prepared to learn and work hard, then I can show you."

The Knight bowed once more and nodded. "I would be delighted to learn. I am a hard worker, and when I have a goal in mind I am determined."

The Knight was true to his word. Once he had fixed his sight upon something, he was the kind of person to see it through. Practical and focused, he proved to be an asset, and enjoyed working with the sisters and learning the secrets of abundance.

In particular, he enjoyed spending time with Charity, and although none of the sisters claimed to be head of the family, it became obvious that she was the driving force, the nurturing power behind the community that they had built. With her huge heart and open mind, it was easy to see why so many loved her, and the Knight soon felt the same. He went out of his way to make her happy and worked even harder in her company, for in his eyes, she was a Queen in waiting.

After some time assisting the sisters and helping with the community, the Knight knew it was time to return to his castle, but he didn't want to leave without Charity. Bending down on one knee, with a hand on his heart, he professed his love and asked her to be his Queen. Although she, too, felt the same, Charity would not leave the home she had created. The Knight knew better than to plead his case and, with a heavy heart, mounted his steed and went on his way.

QUEEN of PENTACLES

QUEEN OF PENTACLES

THEMES

To nurture and
be prosperous

A woman who is
an earth mother

THE KNIGHT WAS MISSED BY ALL THE VILLAGERS, especially by Charity, but even in the depths of her sorrow she could not bring herself to leave the home she had made. Her village, the meadow, and the money tree were all a part of her and she felt such a connection. The earth she stood upon was more than just a platform; it was a living, breathing space, and she had nurtured and cared for it. She planted, sowed, and toiled upon the land and, in return, nature had given her a bountiful supply of crops and gold. Not only that, but the villagers were her friends and family. There was a deep bond that held them together and she was at the heart of it.

As the days moved into weeks, the routine of life continued. The meadow blossomed, the tree grew even bigger, and the entire community felt the benefits of this prosperity. Then one day, out of the blue, a gift arrived. Packaged in sheets of fabric and tied with ribbons, it was enormous. The label held Charity's name written in a hand she recognized; it was from the Knight. Quickly she removed the outer layers to reveal an ornate throne. With intricate carvings along each arm, it was truly a sight to behold, and there was a message to go with it.

"For my Queen. If you will not come to me, I shall come to you," it read.

"Oh, my!" gasped Celine.

"That's lovely!" cried Penny.

Charity simply smiled. Taking a few tentative steps, she lifted herself up onto the seat. It felt so comfortable, as if it had been made for her. Sitting back she felt something press against her skin, and on turning realized it was a gold coin, the gold coin that the Knight had carried when he had first visited. Lovingly she held it in her hands. It was a symbol of his commitment to her and represented the flow of love between them.

In that moment, she felt like a Queen, a nurturing mother, with all of her family around her. The only thing missing was her King.

The villagers cheered at the sight of their beloved Charity on the throne.

"All hail the Queen of Pentacles," one of them cried, and this was followed with even more applause.

"All hail the Queen of Pentacles!" came the call once more, but this time the voice made Charity's heart flutter with excitement. It was the deep, velvety voice of her true love, who sang its song loud and clear above the heads of the gathered crowd.

KING OF PENTACLES

Hᴇ ᴄᴜᴛ ᴀ ᴘᴀᴛʜ ᴛʜʀᴏᴜɢʜ ᴛʜᴇ ᴛʜʀᴏɴɢ ᴏꜰ ᴘᴇᴏᴘʟᴇ, with open arms and smiling eyes. He was the same man who had first visited and won Charity's heart, but there was something different about him, an aura of confidence that seemed to grow the closer he got to his Queen. On reaching her he bowed low and offered his hand.

"If you'll let me, I'd like to join you here in your kingdom. I'd like to be your King."

The words hung in the air between them; they seemed to resonate with light and love, and it felt like the entire crowd was waiting for her response. Finally, Charity rose from her throne and took his hand gently.

"You will always be my King," she said.

The people roared in appreciation, and the King rose to his feet. It seemed that in that one moment he had grown in stature. Each step that he took was solid and disciplined. This was a man with vision, a man who had finally achieved his dream. He was a symbol of wealth and attainment, a King who had nothing to prove because he had everything he needed.

And so it was that Charity married her Knight, and they lived as Queen and King together in harmony with the land, and all those who made it their home. They continued to nurture their crops, and the money tree also thrived and spread, covering so much land that it became a small forest. Abundance flowed throughout the kingdom and beyond, and no one went without.

The sisters Penny and Celine played their part, and were happy to be members of a much bigger community, one where people looked after each other. The gold coin that had started everything now formed the roots of the tree, anchoring it to the earth. The magic it held had spread in many ways and reached so many people, thanks to the lessons the sisters had learned.

Not a million miles away, the old oak stood in the same place, in the same wood. It was home to all manner of creatures, including a curious little man with a pointy hat who sat in his vantage point in the canopy, counting out magical coins. He was marking time, waiting for the next person to lose their way upon the path, in the hope that they might discover the value of a rich and happy life.

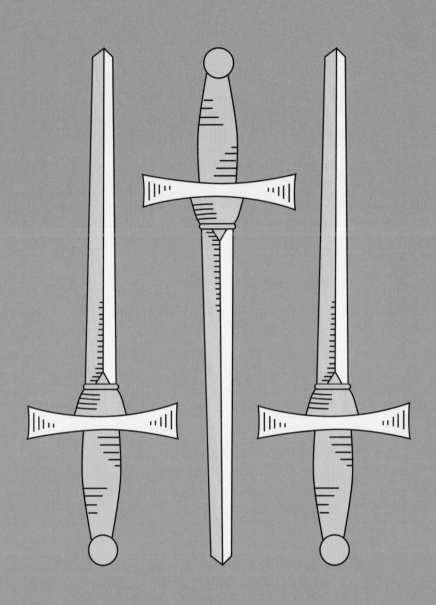

The Suit of Swords

ACE OF SWORDS

THEMES

Action

Passion

A breakthrough
or idea

ONE MORNING, IN A TIME AND A PLACE far from here, a girl called Scarlett woke with a start and shook the blankets from her bed. She took a deep breath to steady her heart—it would not do to wake the Witch at this early hour.

She'd been having a dream; the same one she'd had for many months. It plagued her thoughts in the day and stole her away in the night. It started with a circle of fire taller than the tallest pines in the forest, with her at the center, small and curled into a ball. There was nowhere to run, no way of escape. All she could do was watch as the flames moved closer. Usually she woke before they met and consumed her forever, but tonight's version was different.

The flames licked and curled above her head, the inferno arched over her, and she could feel the heat intensify. Clouds of smoke hovered and filled her lungs, and just when she thought she could breathe no more, something strange happened—a glimmering sword sliced through the smoke, cutting the air in two. The weapon itself was magnificent, the kind that Kings would dream of and only the bravest of warriors could wield. It floated above her head, the sharp end pointing toward the heavens, and there on the tip hung a golden crown, a symbol of power and royalty.

Scarlett didn't need to analyze the dream to know its truth. The meaning was clear to her heart. The crown belonged to her one true love, the King's son, Edmund, and the sword represented her passion for him, its sharp, swift action cutting through the gloom. The fire was her torment at the thought he would be betrothed to another, and that it wasn't meant to be.

"But what am I to do? What can I do?" she whispered to the darkness.

Edmund had never even looked her way, and why should he? She was the Witch's apprentice, a scrap of a girl from the village who spent all her time in the woods gathering herbs for lotions and potions. Her life plan was clear. She would remain at the Witch's side, in the wooden cabin they shared, until the day the old woman died. Then Scarlett would take on the role for herself and become sage and wise woman to all.

But now things were different. The dream had sparked something inside; an idea, an urge to act upon her passion. It had ignited a flame that could not be extinguished and was about to propel her forward to accept her fate.

TWO OF SWORDS

THE WITCH LISTENED AT THE BEDROOM DOOR. She could sense something, a foreboding presence coming from her protégé. Scarlett was a beautiful soul and that's why she'd been the ideal choice to follow in her footsteps, but the girl had so much to learn. She wasn't wise to the ways of the world. There was a weakness there, something that could lead her down a dark path. She didn't have the power to read Scarlett's dreams, but she knew that something was troubling her and that it pulled at her heart.

The big question was what to do next. As Scarlett's mentor she could intervene and advise, keep heartache at bay, and stop her from making a terrible mistake, but then what would the girl learn? How would she ever progress if she didn't stumble? There were others to consider too. The Witch already knew of the feelings Scarlett harbored for

Edmund, and that it could come to no good. He had never shown any interest in her apprentice, and probably never would. He was to be King, and she was to be a Wise Woman; they were not meant to cross paths. Either way, she knew that Scarlett was so consumed with passion she could not see clearly, and would likely do anything to try and ensnare the Prince.

The Witch tiptoed out of the cabin and into the forest. It was still early and there was only a chink of light coming from the crescent moon. She loved the break of dawn; there was so much potential to be had. Nothing was decided as yet, and the day could go in any direction. Quickly and deftly she moved, despite her age. She weaved through the trees and made her way to the lakeside. Here the moon shone a little brighter, casting light upon the water. The Witch took a moment and sat at the water's edge. She drew the blindfold from within her skirts and tied it loosely around her eyes. She knew that it was only without sight that she would truly see and make the right decision. Crossing her arms over her chest, she took a deep breath and drew down the power of the moon.

In this moment she felt distanced from the problem, calm, and able to be objective. Should she be swayed by her heart and help Scarlett see sense and keep her safe from her own judgment, or should she stand back and let matters develop as they most certainly would? In this instance, she felt that her mind should overrule her heart.

It was a double-edged sword that she held in both hands. She had the power to do something, but the decision would not be easy. The Witch released a breath.

"Yes, I see now what must happen," she whispered to the moon— but silence was her only reply.

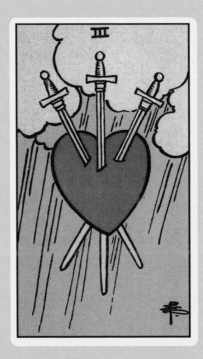

THREE OF SWORDS

THEMES

Heartbreak

Pain

Sorrow

Hurt

ONCE SCARLETT HAD FINISHED HER CHORES for the morning, she always took a break. The Witch allowed her a couple of hours in the middle of the day that she could use for study, or to practice spells. Today, after her dream, she had other ideas. Taking the path through the woods she made her way to the clearing near the entrance, hoping that she had timed it right. Her plan was simple. Edmund went riding with his brothers the same time every week, and they always passed through the woods. She would make him see her, their eyes would meet, and he would fall hopelessly in love. All thoughts of any future betrothed would be gone, replaced by a new flame-haired beauty.

Crouching in amongst the tall grasses, she placed her basket on the ground. It was a ruse, but at least if she gathered herbs the Witch would be pleased, and she had something to show for her time. Here amongst swarthy clumps of rosemary she felt at home. The scent was pungent; no wonder it was said that wherever it grew you'd find a powerful woman.

Just as that thought passed through her head, she heard voices, and the sound of horses' hooves kicking up the dirt and then slowing to a walk. It was Edmund and his brothers. Quickly she smoothed down her apron, pushed a stray hair behind her ears, and stood up.

"Look what we have here!" a voice said; it wasn't Edmund's. "She looks pleased to see you, brother."

"Oh, look at her!" sniggered another younger man. "She's quite pretty if you squint!"

Edmund followed their gaze; his eyes settled briefly on Scarlett.

"Her?" He grimaced. "She's the Witch's girl, probably half mad like the old woman."

Scarlett could feel her cheeks burning. Yes, she'd wanted him to notice her, but not like this.

"What's your name, girl?" he snarled.

Scarlett's lip trembled; she could feel the tears building behind her eyes.

"Well? Cat got your tongue?"

"Come on, let's leave her be. She's not worth your time," said the youngest brother.

Edmund nodded. "Yes, poor wretch. She's definitely not worth it."

And with a brief tug on the reins they were gone, leaving a cloud of dust in their wake.

Scarlett fell to her knees, clutching her chest as an avalanche of tears came. She rocked forward, letting her hands press deep into the earth. It felt like her heart had been pierced from three different directions, torn apart, and broken. Her body shook, and the tears fell into the dirt, into the roots of the rosemary plant. Her heartache was raw, and she couldn't hold back. How could he have been so cruel? The hurtful words he'd said and the way he'd looked at her; it was all too much. She cried for the longest time and when the tears stopped coming, the hate started.

FOUR OF SWORDS

THEMES

Fatigue

Contemplation

Recuperation

Anxiety

Edmund felt exhausted. He'd spent the day hunting with his two brothers, and then feasting in the evening with the other knights. It was hard work wearing a mask, pretending to care about his birth right, when in reality it sickened him. He played a part, and he played it well. His friends didn't really care about him. It was all for show, but he was just as culpable. The role he'd assumed meant that everyone was happy. No more withering looks from his father, no more lectures about his duty and what was expected of him. It was a relief at first, but over time he realized the toll of this falsehood. He had never felt so alone. Lost in solitude, not able to express how he truly felt, it was like being in prison and he desperately longed for escape. He craved release and the freedom that it would bring. To spend some time by himself, learning to be happy in his own skin.

Edmund sighed and lay back in his bed. Plumped up pillows and satin sheets could do nothing for the anguish he felt. Sleep would not come easy—it rarely did. His thoughts turned to the girl in the woods, and how cruel he had been to her. The words he'd spat out, as if saying them made them true. It was unfair and he'd seen their effect, the way her skin colored and her eyes glistened.

He placed his hands together in prayer. "That was not me. It's not who I am. I pray for release from this burden."

There was no answer. If anyone heard his prayer, they kept their thoughts to themselves.

Edmund shivered. If he didn't do something soon, the swords of recrimination would fall and pierce his heart. He couldn't see them, but he could feel their presence, as if they were suspended in the air above him. Were they waiting for the right moment to drop?

The temperature in the room dipped and Edmund tried to relax, to put a halt to this particular chain of thought, but every time he shut his eyes, he saw the red-haired girl and the way her expression changed after he'd spoken to her. How could he have been so nasty? Perhaps she would cast a spell on him, turn him into a toad, or something even more reprehensible? It was surely what he deserved.

Pretending to be something he was not had set in motion a chain of events that could not be stopped, and once the truth was out then the swords would fall. The only thing he could do was hold on to this moment, right now. He took a deep breath in to steady his nerves and tried to find some respite in the darkness.

FIVE OF SWORDS

It was the morning after the night before and Edmund was deeply troubled. He'd spent the night in turmoil and was feeling unsettled. He could not go on living a lie. Something had to be done before it was too late. He needed to speak to his father, to address the kingdom as well and explain that this was not who he was, or what he wanted. With a heavy heart he made his way to the lakeside, in the hope that he would catch his younger brothers, who were normally training at this time in the morning. He would explain the situation to them first. Being his brothers he hoped they would understand and not judge him like the King, but Edmund was wrong.

"You are selfish!"

"Don't you understand the great privilege you have? I would give anything to be you, to be King one day."

"How can you be so stupid? Have you gone mad?"

"The witch from yesterday has surely cast a spell on you!"

The taunts came thick and fast, and they did not stop. Edmund tried to argue his case, but his brothers offered little sympathy. Instead the insults flowed, and he found himself at the center of the conflict.

"When Father finds out he will banish you, and he'll punish the witch for turning your head."

"It is nothing to do with the girl from yesterday. I have been feeling this way for a long time."

"No you haven't. You've changed, brother. You are not in your right mind. The girl has cursed you!"

"She has done nothing wrong; it is I who should pay for how I spoke to her!"

Why were they not listening? How could his own brothers not understand? Anger and bitterness swelled within him, and soon they came to blows. Edmund was by far the more experienced fighter of the three, and found it easy to best the pair, but the win left him feeling hollow. There was no joy in this defeat, for while he was the victor, he had lost something dear to him—his brothers' love and respect. He had lashed out in frustration and done the most awful thing when he should have just walked away. Now everything was destroyed between them. How had it come to this?

Quietly he gathered up the swords and turned his back. There was nothing to be done here. The die had been cast. Word would reach the King of his betrayal to the throne. His fate was sealed.

SIX OF SWORDS

SCARLETT HAD SPENT THE PAST COUPLE OF DAYS in a state of bewilderment. She had never felt so lost or alone, despite the Witch's best efforts to raise a smile and keep her occupied. She had felt so sure that Edmund was the one for her, even though they had never met. She had recognized a fellow soul, sensed it with all her being, and yet it was a fiction, the stuff of daydreams and nothing more. Edmund was not who she thought he was. That day in the woods had changed everything. She had sobbed, and she had raged. She had dug her fingers into the soil and torn up the rosemary by its roots. She had muttered incantations and let her heart bleed into the earth, but now it was time to move on.

To help her make that transition Scarlett would perform a rite of passage, a simple ritual to help her release the past. It was something the Witch had suggested might help, and although she'd been less than keen at the time, in the cold light of day it seemed the only solution. Gathering a small bag of herbs, she made her way to the lake. For the magic to work, she needed free-flowing water.

The serenity of the lake always soothed her mind, and she spent a few minutes simply watching the flow of the water and the boatmen on their rafts as they ferried passengers to the other side. She wished she could join them. How wonderful it would be, to let the pull of the tide transport her to a new life. Instead she must stay, fulfill her duty, and accept what was to be. It wasn't so much of a hardship, quite the opposite—Scarlett loved learning the spells and helping people, and even enjoyed the Witch's company, but sometimes she just wanted to do something for herself.

Scooping up a handful of herbs from her bag, she cast the dried leaves into the lake. "That which holds me back, I now set free. I leave behind the baggage, let it be."

Placing both hands over her heart, she felt a tug within, as if something had been released. All the emotion of the past few days, the swords that cut her to the bone, were gone. She imagined them lined up on a raft and carried over the lake to some place new, just like the people ferried to and fro.

"I let you go, sweet Edmund," she whispered. "It was never meant to be, I see that now."

As she turned to go, she failed to notice the small man with the royal insignia on his tunic, watching from a distance. Dressed for service to the royal family, he was wiry and short, allowing him to take in the scene and remain hidden from her view.

SEVEN OF SWORDS

THEMES

Deception

Betrayal

Lies

Cunning actions

As THE LIGHT OF THE DAY DWINDLED, the man who had been watching Scarlett stepped out of the shadows. He was the King's right-hand man, the person he turned to when he needed to get things done. It was up to him to sort the mess that Edmund and his brothers had created. A rift amongst the royals would be frowned upon, and cause dissention with the people, not to mention Edmund's sudden revolt, so he was looking for a way to resolve everything.

He smiled sneakily. The answer had fallen at his feet. It would be easy to blame Edmund's insanity upon this girl, just as his brothers had suspected. She was the perfect target for such a betrayal. Not only was it commonly known that she spent time with the Witch in the woods, but he had clearly seen her at the lakeside, the scene of the earlier altercation with Edmund. The timing, however, was wrong, since it was after the fight, but a little deception wouldn't hurt. He could turn things around; say he'd seen her performing a spell earlier in the day and that she was putting a curse on the Prince. A few lies about what he had heard and seen would add salt to the wound.

Some might wonder why he would go to all the trouble of concocting such a story, but this way the King would save face. Edmund's behavior could be explained away and eventually he'd be coaxed back to the family fold. The girl would be cast out for using dark magic, but that was really no loss. It was obvious from what the brothers had told him that she had a crush on Edmund and had taken his rebuff in the woods badly. It was all working out brilliantly. The little man congratulated himself on coming up with such a cunning plan.

He looked over his shoulder, suddenly aware that he too might be being watched. When trickery was your currency, suspicion was your constant companion. He had always been aware of this but couldn't help his paranoia. Being underhand came second nature to him. So far, he'd been lucky but one day the tables could turn.

Taking a deep breath he steadied his nerves. It was time to set his plan in motion, to make it known that Edmund had been the victim of witchcraft, and to make the girl his scapegoat.

A sly smile curled his lips. How clever was he? The swords of deception might not be real, but he carried them close to his heart.

EIGHT OF SWORDS

S CARLETT AWOKE TO A COMMOTION OUTSIDE. It was the thundering sound of hooves, then shouting and banging on the cabin door. She could hear the Witch, but she couldn't tell what she was saying. There were footsteps, and her own door swung open. The King's guard circled her.

"You must come with us!" the first guard shouted. "Get up now, and get dressed."

"But why? What's going on?"

"You'll find out," the guard sneered, "and don't be trying any of that hocus pocus on us. It will do you no good, in the long run."

"But I wouldn't! I don't use magic that way."

Scarlett looked to the Witch and then back to the stony-faced guard.

"Go with them," the Witch said gently. "All will be well."

"But I haven't done anything wrong."

The Witch smiled. "I know. It's a misunderstanding, that's all. You will figure it out."

Scarlett sighed. Would she? She had no idea what they wanted with her and she felt trapped. Quickly she dressed, and let the guards lead her out to the waiting coach. The interior was a dark hole, with a wooden bench and barred windows. This was to be her prison for the journey. Glimmers of sunlight offered chinks of light, but the bars were like swords surrounding her.

Scarlett closed her eyes and tried to think of a reason why she was imprisoned in this way. What had she done? The only thing she was guilty of was loving someone who didn't even know she existed. Yes, it was a fiction she'd created in her mind. She realized now that she'd become obsessed with Edmund, and there was no real basis for her feelings. She'd been held captive by a fantasy, and even now she hadn't fully let go of the idea, but she would. The truth was that her work with the Witch was her real passion. It was her calling, and a part of her she couldn't deny. She might dream of another life, but this was the one she had chosen.

As Scarlett sat in the gloomy cabin of the coach, she wondered what would become of her. Why was the King so angry with her, and what would the end result be? More importantly, she wondered if she would ever escape, and make her way back to the life that she loved so much.

NINE OF SWORDS

THEMES

Anxiety

Worry

Fear

Negativity

O N ARRIVAL AT THE CASTLE, Scarlett was taken to the dungeon and thrown into a small, stone room. There she was held in place on a wooden stool, while they chopped away her curls, leaving her with a boyish crop of hair. This, they said, would dampen the fire of her witchcraft.

The space itself was suffocating. There was a tiny barred window above her head, which offered little light and a glimpse of the outside world if she stood on her bed, on tiptoes. She shivered, not so much from the cold as from the chill that had settled in her heart. Something was very wrong. She slumped down on the bed. The mattress was thin and well worn, and there was no pillow, but it would have to do. She didn't know how long she'd be in this awful place.

She lay down and closed her eyes, gripped her fists tightly and tried to steady her heartbeat. No matter how hard she tried, she could not stop the feeling of dread that was growing in her belly. It crawled up through her rib cage, snaking up her throat and into the space behind her eyes. Anxiety took hold and filled her mind with terrible images of what might be. Were they going to punish her for being so brazen as to think she loved the Prince? Perhaps they planned to cast her out, to banish her from the kingdom for good? Or maybe her punishment would be far worse? She bit her lip, and the bitter taste of blood filled her mouth.

She tried to bring to mind happier times spent in the Witch's company, days when she'd explored the woods and learned about the plants and trees. She thought of healing rituals they'd performed together for the sick, and how she'd seen the infirm transform before her eyes, through the use of her power. She tried to remind herself of all the good things she'd accomplished so far, but it was to no avail. Worry had set in and with it a panic that could not be quelled.

Just as she was plunging deeper into a downward spiral of thought, there was a sound above her head, a tapping, rattling sound that caught her attention. She scrambled to her feet and stretched as far as she could to bring her face to the iron bars. There on the other side, looking down with concern, was a face she knew well.

"Prince Edmund!"

"My lady," he seemed nervous, "I'm sorry for how I talked to you in the woods the other day."

"Is that why I'm here? Why are they holding me?"

"I don't know, but I'll find out."

"I've done nothing wrong, not that I can think of. . . ."

Edmund nodded. "I know. It's me they're angry with. I will get you out of here, I promise."

With that he was gone, and Scarlett was left to her dark thoughts once more.

TEN OF SWORDS

IT WAS SHORTLY BEFORE DAWN when Scarlett was pulled from her dank cell into the main hall of the castle. A crowd had assembled, and she was ordered to kneel on the stone floor while they jeered. In front of her sat Edmund's two brothers, holding council. They looked down at her, an amused expression on their faces. To their right, a small weasel-faced man stood. His thin lips glistened with spittle and every so often he'd lean over and whisper to the brothers.

Eventually the eldest of the pair stood and took a step toward Scarlett.

"You are accused of using the dark arts to put a curse on my brother, Prince Edmund. What do you have to say for yourself?"

Scarlet shivered. "It's untrue. I wouldn't do such a thing!"

"Liar!" the weasel-faced man cried. "I saw you at the lakeside, casting a spell."

"That wasn't a spell, it was a harmless ritual meant for none but me."

"I heard you, you called out the Prince's name, and you wished him to lose his mind. I heard everything you said."

Scarlett shook her head. "No, no, that's not right at all. I didn't say any of that."

"Then why has my brother suddenly denounced his birth right? Why has he fled the castle? He would not do such a thing if he were in his right mind."

Scarlett stared at the floor, and then at the weasel-faced man, who was grinning.

"You've made all this up! Why would you do that? I haven't done anything wrong."

The little man rubbed his hands together. "See how she lies. Something must be done with her, an example made."

Scarlett could feel the panic rising in her chest. She could hardly breathe, and there was nothing she could do to change her fate. It was her word against theirs and she didn't stand a chance. It felt like she'd been pierced ten times, stabbed in the back by blunt swords. The pain was unbearable. If she had any magic in her, now was the time to use it, but she felt defeated. Her life as she knew it was over.

Taking a long, slow gulp of air, she made a wish. A simple request, made with a few words in her head that no one would ever hear.

"Let this be over."

Then, in a heartbeat, she crumpled to the floor. Her limp body sagged as she took her last breath.

PAGE of SWORDS.

PAGE OF SWORDS

THERE WAS A GREAT COMMOTION as the crowd realized what had happened. Cries of "The witch is dead!" could be heard echoing through the vast hall. Then to add to the confusion, the door at the far end burst open. It was Edmund.

He strode to the front of the hall and immediately swept Scarlett up in his arms.

"What have you done?" he asked his brothers. "She is innocent. She didn't put any kind of curse on me!"

Laying her gently on the bench, he tried desperately to resuscitate her but she remained motionless, all color drained from her face. Eventually Edmund turned and addressed the crowd of courtiers and his brothers. His tone, despite being overwrought, was strong and purposeful and he spoke with an eloquence that no one had heard before.

"I was born into this family, and it is an honor to play the role I have been given, but it is not for me. It is not in my heart. I don't want to be King. That doesn't mean I don't respect my family or my father. It is just not the life I choose. I want to make my own way in the world, to express myself freely and with passion. I have tried to do my duty, but it only made me bitter, because deep down it's not what I want. I almost didn't recognize myself. I was cruel and full of hate." He turned then to look at Scarlett.

"This girl was a victim of my anger. I spoke harshly to her; I was rude, and she deserved better. She did nothing to change my mind or trick me. If anything, it was the guilt I felt for being so cruel that made me realize I need to be true to myself. You were all wrong for judging her, and now her death is on your hands."

The hall was silent, and not a breath could be heard amongst the shocked faces. Slowly the truth dawned upon each one. They listened to Edmund's message, and they understood there was no crime, except the one they had created.

"I'm so sorry, brother."

"Me too, please forgive me."

Both brothers were standing now.

"What can we do?"

Edmund shook his head. "You have done enough. You didn't let me explain, but then perhaps I too was at fault. I didn't have the words then to help you understand."

"He told us lies," said the brothers, pointing to the small man who was skulking in the shadows.

"And you believed them," said Edmund softly.

Carefully, he scooped up Scarlett and headed for the door. The crowd watched him go in silence. At last they understood his message. He had expressed himself with crystal clarity, and there was nothing more to be said.

KNIGHT of SWORDS.

KNIGHT OF SWORDS

THEMES

Motivation

Focus

Success

A driven man with
a mission

Speed was of the essence, and Edmund was well aware that time was against him, but he had to try and save Scarlett. No matter what it took he would travel to the ends of the earth in search of a way to bring her back. For the first time in his life, he felt like a man on a mission. He had to succeed; there was no other outcome. She was in this mess because of him and while he couldn't tell if she were truly dead or in some kind of deep sleep, her plight was his doing.

Edmund's horse was fast, one of the quickest in the land, and today it flew through the streets, out toward the fields, along the lakeside, and deep into the heart of the woods. He needed help and there was only one person who could save her. Plundering through the undergrowth, he used his sharp sword to slice at the overhead branches. He dipped and dived holding Scarlett close, as his horse galloped with the wind at its heels. Nothing would stop him from reaching his destination. He had never felt more determined or focused.

Up ahead he could see the small wooden cabin in amongst the tall pines. Before he even reached the door, it was open and the Witch was ushering them inside.

"Here, lay her on the table," she said.

"How did you know we were coming?"

"Sssh!" the Witch said, placing a finger to her lips. "You have done what you needed to do. Now it's up to me."

Edmund stood back; his hands clasped to his lips in prayer.

Please, he willed silently. *Please let her live.*

The Witch placed both hands upon Scarlett's chest. She closed her eyes and muttered some words under her breath. To Edmund, it sounded like she was speaking a foreign language. Quickly she reached for a jar from the ledge and removed the lid.

"Rosemary," she said, looking Edmund in the eye. "The herbs she collected on the day you first met."

She placed a sprig in Scarlett's lifeless hand and curled her fingers around it.

Edmund shuddered as he recalled the memory of how he'd talked to her on that day in the woods.

"I'm so sorry, Scarlett," he said. "With all the power I have, I wish you could hear me say it."

A faint breeze grazed his cheek as he said the words and, suddenly, quite out of the blue, Scarlett took a breath and opened her eyes.

QUEEN OF SWORDS

IT SEEMED LIKE MAGIC IN THAT MOMENT that Scarlett awoke, and perhaps it was, for as she rose from the table there was a sparkle in her eye that had not been there before. The Witch placed a hand on her shoulder and smiled.

"How do you feel?"

Scarlett looked from Edmund to the Witch and then took a breath. "I feel good. I feel renewed, like I have been in a deep sleep and now at last I am awake and revived."

"I thought you were dead," whispered Edmund.

"I was, in a way, but now I've been reborn, and I feel stronger. I'm ready to embrace my true purpose."

The Witch steered her by the arm to a chair in the corner of the room.

"Take a moment and sit. Gather your breath."

As Scarlett sat, she mused on the events of the past few days. It seemed that in a short space of time she had been through so much. She had learned a lot, too, from her experiences. Even the time lost in slumber had helped her see what was really in her heart.

"I was a girl a few days ago, but now I am a woman, in control of my own world. I know what I want and what matters, and it is not a silly fantasy that can never be. I have a calling and a power deep within that I need to use for good."

Edmund walked forward and bowed low at her feet. "You are indeed a Queen of your own making, and I am truly sorry for my part in all this. I too have learned the value of things. I am not that person who you saw in the woods. Please forgive me."

"There is nothing to forgive," smiled Scarlett.

She turned then to face the Witch, who was watching from the shadows.

"You have taught me many things. You have encouraged me and tried to open my eyes to the magic I have within, and I never really appreciated any of it. I saw it as something I had to do, a chore, when in fact it is the one thing I love. It is my soul's purpose to be like you. From now on I will be a diligent student, for it is an honor to spend time with you."

The Witch nodded. "And I with you. We can teach each other."

"And what about you, Prince Edmund?" Scarlett asked. "I can see the change in you too."

"It is a change of heart I have had. I don't want to follow in my father's footsteps, I don't want to rule and become like the rest of my family."

"Then don't," said the Witch. "There are many ways to be a King, without being a tyrant."

Offering a hand to the Prince, she said, "Come, let us help you find your way."

KING OF SWORDS

THEMES

Truth

Authority

Wisdom

Respect

A masterful man

Over the next few weeks Edmund spent a great deal of time with Scarlett and the Witch, learning the ways of the land and how to grow and cultivate all manner of plants and herbs, understanding the role that nature plays in daily life. He immersed himself in the environment and enjoyed spending time with the locals. As his wisdom grew so did his confidence, and he stepped into his power. The need to help his people and create a better world for them became the driving force behind his actions and he realized that there was a place for him, and a purpose.

He began mending fences with his friends and family, communicating his message, and expressing himself with such passion that his brothers accepted the change in him. His father the King was not as easily swayed, but over time even he saw that Edmund was much happier following his own path. He realized that there was more than one way to rule a kingdom, and that the old ways could blend with the new, to create a more harmonious and productive community.

While Edmund didn't want to sit on the throne, he did want to help his people and bridge the gap between peasant and nobleman. He wanted to be the voice of those who normally went unheard, and to speak out on their behalf. As a guide and a mentor, he would be there for them, offering advice and expressing their needs whenever he could. Edmund would act as conduit between the people and their King and help to build on that relationship.

Scarlett, too, played her role by providing a sounding board to his ideas, talking things through, and using her scrying ability to help him see a way forward. She advised him, and in return he encouraged her and watched as her powers blossomed. While her magic grew strong and true, it wasn't the only thing that flourished. The affection they had for each other bloomed into a tangible friendship, based on genuine warmth and respect.

What had started as a fiction, a spark of passion that burned within a young girl's heart, had become a meeting of minds, a platonic pairing that would stay strong forever. The irony was not lost on the Witch, who had watched their relationship develop with interest.

"You are truly the Queen of the Witches, my dear," she said one day, as they walked along the lakeside. "You have manifested all that you wished for and now you have your King as your closest friend."

"Perhaps it was always meant to be," added Scarlett.

"Perhaps," said the Witch, smiling, and they walked on in companionable silence.

The Suit of Cups

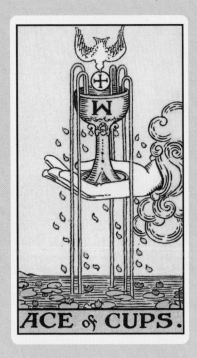

ACE OF CUPS

THEMES

Love

Purity

Fulfillment

Fertility

ONCE UPON A TIME MIGHT BE A GOOD PLACE to start this tale, but any moment in time can be special, given the right circumstances. A moment is what you make of it. For some it is the start of something, the birth of an emotion, a feeling that rises within and consumes the heart. Of course it can also be a real birth, the spark of life that grows into a beautiful flame if it is fed, watered, and loved. And so it was, in the case of this particular story, for this is an emotional tale and one that should take you on a journey.

It started with a cry, plaintive and shrill. It cut through the morning air and attracted the attention of a kindly gentleman out for an early stroll by the river. He wasn't expecting anything to penetrate his thoughts this day, for he was heavy in heart and mind, but this sound called to him deeply. On further investigation he discovered the source was coming from the water's edge. He followed the trail of noise and discovered a tiny babe, wrapped in muslin and lace, and nestled upon a lotus leaf.

"Oh, my!" he cried. "Look at you, little one, aren't you a beauty!"

And in that one isolated moment, he fell in love.

He never questioned where the infant had come from, what her background was, or who she belonged to. It didn't seem strange that she simply floated into his life and turned it around. To him, that moment by the river was the start of her story. She was love personified and his cup overflowed.

In her tiny fingers she held so much potential. He could almost imagine the life she would have, and sometimes when he closed his eyes, he would picture it. He would see her as a girl playing in the garden, the joy in her eyes as she chased a butterfly or smelled the sweet scent of a rose in bloom. As a young woman she would be beautiful, a prize to behold, and a sweetheart to many, but to one special person she would be everything and they would begin a new life together. Then he'd picture her as a woman with her own tiny babe in arms, a content look in her eye as she nurtured the child. And so the story went on and he watched her grow to fruition.

All of this he saw in that one moment and, as he picked her up and cradled her for the first time, he felt the true nature of love.

TWO OF CUPS

THEMES

Unity

Harmony

Balance

Soul mates

THE BABY SOON GREW INTO A BEAUTIFUL YOUNG GIRL called Lily and she was the apple of her father's eye. Full of lightness and love, she could see the joy in everything and the relationship they shared was truly special. Her father adored her, and in him she saw the kind of man who one day she would like to be with. The values he instilled in her were fair and true, from honesty and loyalty to the ability to empathize with others and see their point of view. Lily was a shining example of sweetness to all around.

Most of all though, she treasured the relationship she had with her father. Every day they'd share a moment in the gardens, and have a meeting of minds where they would talk and laugh. He'd recount the tales of his youth, and she would listen and learn from his experiences.

"I do so love these moments with you, Father," she would say, and he would smile and nod.

"They are indeed special. You are special, and one day you will find someone who sees in you what I see in you."

"A true love?"

"A soul mate, my dear."

"And what is that?" she would ask, and he would raise his cup and say, "Someone you connect with at the deepest level. Someone who recognizes what's in here," and he would tap his chest lightly.

"A friend?"

"Yes, your best friend, someone you can rely on, a rock, but also someone who makes your heart sing."

Lily would study her father's face and see an echo in his features of something that had been lost a long time ago. There was sadness, but there was also so much joy at the thought of this person.

"Did you have that once?" she would ask, and he would gaze off into the distance, as if caught in memory.

"Yes, my dear, I did."

Lily would sigh, and place a hand on her father's shoulder, for she could sense the sorrow but also the deep love that he had once had. And while she didn't understand it fully yet, she hoped one day she would meet that special someone who she connected with—the person who could make her heart sing.

But for now she found contentment and harmony in the world around her. For now, every relationship, from family to friendship, filled her with happiness.

THREE OF CUPS

THEMES

Friendship

Celebration

Camaraderie

Togetherness

THE DAYS MOVED INTO WEEKS and then months, and soon it was Lily's coming-of-age birthday, a big event that would be marked by everyone in the kingdom. Her father had planned a great feast, a coming together of all the families in the region. There would be fun and games, and lots of dancing, for there was nothing Lily loved more than taking to the floor and spinning around to music.

While Lily did not have sisters to share this special moment with, she did have lots of friends and everyone wanted to be there to celebrate with her. The build-up to the big day was exciting, and all of the townsfolk joined in, decorating the streets and buildings with ribbons and flowers. The town's square was a hive of activity and there was a general feeling of anticipation. Good things were coming, and spirits were high.

Lily was beside herself, so full of life and keen to move on to the next chapter. It was time for her to find her feet, to step out into the world and discover her true calling. In her mind she knew that, deep down, she wanted to find a soul mate to share this journey with, but how easy would that be?

Her father made it sound like a once-in-a-lifetime love, and if that was the case, then the chances of meeting that special someone were few and far between. It was highly unlikely that they would just stroll into her life, or that they would by chance meet one day on the street. It seemed to her that she would have to actively search for this person and do all she could to find her love. This puzzled Lily, for she wasn't sure where to start looking, and she would often question her two closest girl friends on the subject.

"How do you find the one? Where on earth do you start?" she would ask, and they would grin and look at each other in a knowing way.

"Oh, Lily," replied the older of the two, whose name was Rose, "it will happen when it happens."

"You can't force these things," said Violet, her sister.

"But what if it never happens?" asked Lily.

"Stop worrying and start enjoying yourself. You have plenty of time for romance," said Rose.

That was always the answer, and it was true, she did, so when the day of her birthday arrived Lily enjoyed every moment.

She sang and danced with her two best friends. They raised their cups in celebration and cheered and laughed together. She reveled in the attention and felt truly grateful for all of the love in her life. Lily realized she was blessed and enjoyed making merry with her nearest and dearest.

FOUR OF CUPS

WHILE LILY WAS ENJOYING HER BIRTHDAY FEAST, across the valley, sitting high on the mountain was a young man in a very different frame of mind. Lost in thought, he failed to notice the beautiful blue sky above his head, or the tree that towered over him, providing shade from the blazing sun. He failed to see much of anything, for he was weighed down by his own feelings.

To this young man, at this exact moment, life seemed dull and without opportunity. Despite his best efforts, he felt that he was not making progress in any area. The dissatisfaction was growing inside of him, and it was hard to see a way forward. Yes, he'd had offers, chances that perhaps he should have taken, but in truth, they didn't feel right. He was searching for something, but he didn't know what.

His arms were folded and his legs were crossed, creating a barrier to change, but he didn't notice. Before him he'd lined up three cups; each one represented a path, or a choice; it was another failed attempt at progress. Nothing was going his way. So steeped in his own woe was he that he failed to notice the cup that was offered behind him. A whisper of opportunity that came on the breeze, from a distant land over the valley.

If he'd been fully aware and engaged in the moment, he might have felt it, the need to roam and stretch his legs, to move in the direction of the wind. Instead, he remained rooted to the spot, head hung low, immersed in his own apathy.

He wondered if he should just give up, go back home, and lead an unremarkable life like so many others. It was surely the right course of action; but something inside of him stirred. He had to break free of this rut that he found himself in. He had to find a deeper meaning, and a calling. His heart fluttered as the faint hint of adventure entered his mind. Could it be that all he needed to do was take that first step, trust in the power of the Universe and his own magic, and embrace the unknown without worrying so much?

He looked about him. He looked out beyond the valley and wondered what lay ahead. What would he find if he were to stride out in that direction? There could be more of the same, or perhaps he would find something worth holding on to. As weary as he felt, something inside would not let him give up, so with some reluctance and trepidation he stumbled to his feet.

FIVE OF CUPS

I T HAD BEEN A FEW DAYS SINCE LILY'S BIRTHDAY celebrations, and while the town returned to a calmer state, there was a somber change in her personal circumstances. Her father had taken ill, and being of an advanced age, was getting weaker by the day. Lily, being the dutiful and devoted daughter, never left his side. She employed all of the best healers and medics in the kingdom in a bid to make him better, but nothing worked. Every night she would read to him, and every day she would wipe his brow and tell him her dreams, in the hope that it would ignite a spark of life, but by the end of the second week her worst fears came true. Her father passed away from the land of living, leaving Lily alone and heartbroken.

Her sorrow was all consuming. She had never experienced grief, and it swept over her like a river of pain.

To lose the one person who meant so much was more than she could cope with. She had always known the origins of her tale, and how her father had found her that day by the river, but it had never mattered. He was her family. He was her love, and now she had lost him.

Friends and family tried to console her. They gathered about her like a great cloak, providing words of comfort, but nothing helped. All warmth was gone from her life, snuffed out when her father took his last breath. Her two closest friends, Rose and Violet, did their best but even they could not reach poor Lily.

"Your father would not want this," they would urge. "He would want you to move on and find happiness."

Her reply was always the same. "How can I move on? I can't let go of the pain, not yet."

And then the tears would flow, and the loneliness would take over.

Lily felt completely isolated, distanced from life. She found it hard to regain the sense of joy and lightness that had always been such a part of her.

As the days drifted into weeks, she wondered if she would ever find her way out of the darkness. But as with all things, life moves on day by day, and slowly but surely Lily began to put one foot in front of the other once more. She began to focus less on her loss, and more on what she had gained from the years she had spent with her father. There appeared a chink of light in the distance, and Lily reached out and grasped it.

SIX OF CUPS

I N THE DAYS THAT FOLLOWED Lily began to think more about where she had come from. What had brought her into the arms of her loving father? It wasn't that she wanted to know her real parents, but she did want to understand who she really was. Her father had always been open and had told her the truth from a young age. He'd made it a fun storytelling game, where they would guess her true identity and make up magical stories together.

As these thoughts of her childhood consumed her, Lily became more intrigued, and this curiosity helped to soothe her grief. Her father had explained how he'd found her wrapped in muslin and lace, cradled in a lotus flower. She knew where those flowers grew, and that there was a town close by—perhaps this was the place of her birth? There was only one way to find out, and Lily was determined.

She packed a bag of her dearest belongings, including the muslin and lace wrap that had kept her warm as a tiny babe, and began the journey to what she hoped would be her true home. It took her almost two days by foot, but the radiant sunshine and blue skies put a spring in her step, and she spent that time reliving happy childhood moments. She missed her father dearly, but at least she had the memories, and she could call on them at any time.

When she finally reached the small town, it was the morning of the third day and the townsfolk were setting up ready for market. Slowly she meandered through the cobbled streets, wondering if this was a path her real parents had taken. Had they, too, strolled hand in hand, down the same road, or was this a place they had passed through to reach their final destination?

For a moment she stopped by a flower stall to admire the pretty blooms, and that's when she recognized the distinctive-shaped petals of the lotus in amongst the bunches.

"Here, these are for you," said the young flower boy, passing her a blossom-filled cup.

"Oh, they're beautiful, but I couldn't. I have no money."

"They're a gift," he smiled.

"They remind me of my childhood, or at least the tales my father would tell me."

"Then you really must take them." He nodded, removing the cup from the row at his feet.

Lily expressed her thanks and held the cup close to her chest. It warmed her heart and soul, and made her realize that nothing is ever forgotten, or lost.

SEVEN OF CUPS

THE YOUNG MAN HAD FINALLY DESCENDED the mountain and put his apathy behind him. He, too, was traveling in the direction of the same town as Lily. With every step he took, he felt more alive and open to possibility. His head was no longer weighed down with thoughts of failure; instead it was in the clouds, daydreaming about what could be. There were so many options available to him. Why could he not see that before? It was as if the sky had suddenly cleared, to reveal a cluster of wishes that he could make real—but which one to try first?

Should he start his own business? Learn a skill or a trade? Try his hand with Lady Luck and make a fortune gambling? Seek a mentor to help? Find a place to live or build one? The questions tumbled through his mind, until he felt his head might explode, and worsened when he entered the town.

It was market day, and the streets were lined with stalls of every description. There were tables laden with fruit and vegetables, baked goods, sweet treats, cakes, and so many biscuits. The sugary aroma made his stomach rumble. There were tables dripping in jewelry, crystals, and colored stones, and stalls selling garments, from cloaks and dresses to reams of material that could be cut to any size or shape. There were tables groaning with plants and wreaths, those that sold herbs, and eyecatching flower displays. There were even stalls that sold curious creatures; lizards and snakes, and animals he didn't have the name for and had never seen in his life. It was a feast for the eyes, and quite overwhelming.

He didn't know where to look, or what to choose. The vendors did their best to reel him in with sales talk and quips, offers, and trades that all sounded too good to be true. His mind was spinning as he made his way along the crooked slabs. It felt like he had wandered into a fantasy world, and that all of it was an illusion.

"How do I decide what I want? How do I make a choice? It's all so confusing," he muttered to himself.

If only there was a way to find some clarity. It seemed that he had gone from one state of being to another, and yet still he did not know his true purpose.

He looked to the heavens for a sign, raising his hands in the air as if reaching for inspiration. That's when he saw her—a woman so fair, she took his breath away. In that moment, all other thoughts vanished from his head.

EIGHT OF CUPS

THE YOUNG MAN WAS ENTRANCED by the dark-haired girl. He watched as she moved through the crowds of people, a cup of flowers clutched to her chest. Her curls spilled about her shoulders, catching the sunlight.

"Who is she?" he asked the nearest vendor, but the man simply shrugged and turned away. By the time the young man glanced back, the girl was nowhere to be seen.

"No!" he cried. He had to find her. Standing on tiptoes he peered through the mass of people, searching for any movement, for just the briefest glimpse up ahead. He pushed and shoved his way through the crowds, heading down the hill, but still there was no sight of her. "Have you seen her? Did you see the girl carrying the cup?" he asked every vendor along the path. The answer was always the same, a flat no, or a blank face.

He picked up speed, running as fast as he could despite the people in his way, which only served to annoy those in front of him.

He stared in store windows, took detours down the side streets in the hope that she had done the same, but the outcome never changed. In the end he decided to tail back the way he had come, and double check that he hadn't missed her. Perhaps she had slipped by unnoticed, although he knew it was highly unlikely. She was all he could see, and all he could think about. He knew his behavior was untoward, and totally out of character. Moments before, his head had been full of hot air and he'd been bewildered by the choices in front of him. Now, everything had changed. There was something about her; the minute he saw her he knew they were meant to continue on this journey together.

The young man was a dreamer, with the soul of poet. He was easily distracted and sensitive to the ways of the world, but he knew this girl was special. In her he recognized a fellow soul, and that had to count for something.

Around and around he went in his search for her. Minutes turned into hours, and the streets all looked the same. The crowds diminished and the day turned into night. The vendors dwindled, the stores closed, and still he waited. In truth, he felt trapped. He could not go anywhere for fear that she was still here and there was a chance to meet, but by the same token, while he waited, she could have moved on to the next town. He didn't know what to do for the best. Darkness took hold of the sky, and also his thoughts. He could feel the icy fingers of disappointment wrap around his heart. He had to accept that she had gone, to let the dream go. Slowly, he made his way to the town gate. It was time to abandon this course of action, to withdraw and move on.

NINE OF CUPS

THEMES

Dreams come true

Fulfillment

Contentment

Abundance

Time passed quickly for Lily and the young man, but in different ways. Lily, for her part, continued her quest to find out who she really was, and on the day of the market, struck lucky. While the townsfolk had gathered to buy and sell their wares, it gave her the ideal opportunity to ask questions, and those questions soon led to a discovery and her sudden disappearance. Talk of a beautiful maiden with a unique birth story soon reached powerful ears, and Lily was swiftly whisked away to an opulent manor on the other side of the town, where the truth was revealed.

At first, she couldn't quite believe the tale she'd been told, but she couldn't deny it stirred something in her. A rich family with a young daughter, betrothed to a man who she hadn't even met, yet in love with another much poorer soul. Their love had been true and their union brief, for when the girl fell pregnant he was sent away, and the affair hushed up. Once the babe had been born, they wrapped her in muslin and lace and left her by the river. The girl, Lily's real mother, was desperately ill after giving birth and had no knowledge of what had happened to her infant. She'd spent years since trying to find her but had died before that dream could be realized. Her only son from the arranged marriage was determined to carry out her wishes and continue the search. And so it was revealed that Lily had a brother and a whole new family who welcomed her into their lives wholeheartedly.

They invited her into their home and she soon settled. In fact she thrived, for the knowledge of who she was had imbued her with power and hope. The love she received from her father would always be with her; now she had formed new bonds and this lifted her heart. She governed the household and became a part of the community, giving back and advising those in need. She flourished and prospered, and for the first time felt truly fulfilled.

It was a dream come true to have discovered her family, to be accepted with such warmth and affection, and while she never forgot her previous life, she knew that this was where she was meant to be.

Although her brother sat at the heart of the family and the head of the table, he was more than just her benefactor; he offered brotherly love and support too. She felt like the richest person in the kingdom, to have been so lucky and have two such wonderful and loving families, and this gratitude brought even more blessings to her door.

TEN OF CUPS

THEMES

Divine love

Bliss

Fairy-tale endings

Harmony

THE YOUNG MAN HAD ALSO FOUND HIS PLACE in the world. In a neighboring town, he took up an apprenticeship with a local artist. At first, he would simply assist the older man, clearing and cleaning his brushes and tools, preparing each canvas, but as time went on it became clear that he also had some creative talent, and it became his passion. He never forgot the dark-haired girl, and how she had pulled at his heart strings, but instead of dwelling upon those feelings he put them into his work. He invested his time and energy and had a clear goal in mind.

It made him smile to think of how far he had come. No longer was he the confused daydreamer, the boy with no plan who could not see farther than his nose. Now he was a man whose life had meaning, and he took great joy from his work.

One day, having made quite a reputation for his paintings, he was called upon to create a special picture, one that would represent divine love in its many guises. It was an interesting commission from a wealthy family in the next town, and he was keen to do his best. With this in mind he decided to visit the family, and learn more about them, for this would help him in his work. And so it was that the young man finally met Lily, for the painting had been her idea, and in that moment, everything changed for both of them.

Lily had often pondered on her father's words, and how he had spoken of a soul mate for her. She had mused on the subject from time to time, and although she had many suitors, not one of them made her heart sing. She had wondered if it would ever happen, but being content in her life, she had kept the thought tucked away until that fateful day.

When their eyes met for the first time, something very special happened. It was a meeting of minds and souls, and the stirring within did indeed cause her heart to sing. The more she talked to the young man, the more she realized that he was what she had been searching for, and the feeling was mutual.

Days turned into weeks, and they spent almost every waking hour together. The young man decided that he should paint his portrait in Lily's garden, to be close to her and to feel inspired.

Eventually it was time for the final artwork to be revealed. Family and friends gathered in anticipation, along with the young man's mentor, who had journeyed to see his commission. As the curtain fell, gasps of amazement could be heard. The picture was a triumph—ten cups set in rainbow arc of color; beneath it children played, and a couple rejoiced at the scene. It was a true representation of the power of love, from a family united in harmony to the divine love that Lily and her beau had found in each other. But another revelation was at hand. The artist who had nurtured the young man's talent had another reason for being there. In truth, he had followed the family with interest for many years, and now that Lily had been found, he could reveal his true identity as her father. The two were reunited, the family was complete, and love flowed freely between them all.

PAGE OF CUPS

THEMES

An inquisitive child

Daydreamer

Spirituality

Psychic gifts

LILY WED HER YOUNG MAN IN THE SPRING of the following year, with her family and her birth father at her side, and in the summer of the year after, gave birth to their first child. This beautiful dark-haired boy was to be their best creation yet, for he had eyes the color of summer skies, and an open and enquiring mind. Everything excited him, and each day brought new adventures.

Lily soon learned that the world looked a very different place through the eyes of her son. Gifted in the psychic arts, the boy could see beyond the veil and had a wisdom beyond his years. He instinctively knew things that could not be explained and would often announce something that had not yet happened but would come into being in the following weeks. He was sensitive, too, and able to pick up on the needs of others.

As a small child he would enter a room and read the atmosphere. He was also drawn to people because of their energy, and if someone was in need of cuddle, he was there to deliver. Lily marveled at this empathy that came naturally to her son.

"He is special," she would tell her husband. "He has a gift."

"He has many gifts," her beau would agree, "and he is just starting out. I can see great things for him. He is a dreamer like I once was."

And it was true that as the child grew into a young boy, he had a head full of ideas and aspirations. Most important of all, he wanted to learn about everything. Everywhere he went he asked questions, probed the minds of the most learned of men and sought answers. He asked Lily to take him to the churches and synagogues, to the chapels and the burial sites, so that he could understand more about his ancestors and what they believed. He spent hours perusing the shelves in the library and devoured some of the ancient texts. And when he wasn't studying, he would be out and about, seeking new places and faces to feed his thirst for knowledge.

Lily marveled at the miracle that was her boy. She taught him everything her father had shared with her, and more. Her husband also showed the boy how to draw and paint, how to observe, and then respond to what he had seen in his own unique way. It wasn't surprising then when the boy literally saw things that others could not, from faces in the shadows to a talking fish in his drinking cup. Her son had the power to see the unseen.

And while Lily's son wanted to know how the world worked, he never lost his sense of wonder. Life to him was magical and he loved every minute of it.

KNIGHT OF CUPS

KNIGHT of CUPS

THEMES

Romance

Charm

Following your heart

A chivalrous gentleman

By THE TIME LILY'S SON REACHED ADULTHOOD, he was a fine-looking and intelligent man. His handsome face was framed with charcoal curls and his eyes were cornflower blue and full of sparkle. Popular with the townsfolk, he was often called "Prince Charming" and not just because of his looks. His manner was gentle and caring, and he was known for his chivalrous behavior, but while many a maiden tried to win his heart, none truly set it alight. It wasn't that he was being hard to please but, like his mother, he was waiting for something special, someone who could make his heart sing.

And so it was that on a beautiful morning in the spring, he packed his bags and donned his finest armor in preparation for a journey. He needed to make his own way in the world, to find his purpose and his true love, and he couldn't do that where he was.

"We must let him go," Lily's husband said, placing an arm around her shoulders.

"He is doing exactly what we did at his age. He needs to step out on his own and find the path that is right for him."

Lily nodded. "It's true, I followed my heart and so did you, and it brought us together. Love is the key to everything."

It was a sentiment she echoed to her first born as he mounted his silver-gray steed.

"Go gently son, and always follow your heart. You are a Knight now, and you must embrace this new stage in your life."

The Knight left his home and all that was familiar, and headed into the unknown. He rode steadily, for he was not in a race. He wanted to enjoy every moment. Making his way past the river, which ran the length of his kingdom and into the next, he followed the flow of the water. His emotions were charged, and he was full of anticipation.

He traveled for weeks and months and, during the many encounters he had, he met one such soul who did indeed make his heart sing loudly. When she saw him, she too was smitten, but little did the handsome Knight know there was more to this maiden than first appearances. In truth, she was the Queen of her kingdom. Many suitors had tried to win her heart, but none who recognized her true worth—the treasure that can only shine from within. And so, shedding her royal garb, she had ventured out into the city streets, just a face amongst the crowd, and it was there that they met and fell in love.

The Knight, being ruled by his emotions, had expressed his affection openly with no knowledge of her true identity, and when the truth was finally revealed, it made little difference. He let his love flow freely, like water from a golden cup.

QUEEN of CUPS.

QUEEN OF CUPS

THE QUEEN RULED HER KINGDOM from a throne by the sea. A kind and nurturing leader, she would reflect upon every decision and take it to heart, and so she did with the Knight's proposal of marriage. As much as she loved him, she would always do what was best for her people. Luckily though, she could see that this man was good to the core and, like her, sensitive to the emotions of others. And so it was that they were to be wed in a glorious ceremony, which she would share with the rest of the kingdom. Such an event it was claimed to be that news soon spread of the forthcoming union, and before long Lily came to learn of her son's betrothal.

"We must go and meet our son's bride, and welcome her to the family with open arms," she urged her husband, and he agreed.

They packed their bags, and took to the road once more, only this time together. They followed the path by the river, just as the Knight had done before them, taking their time to enjoy the journey and each other's company. They let the flow of their emotions and the water at their feet lead them straight to the Queen's kingdom. Once within the gated walls, they found their way to the castle.

The Queen was delighted by their presence and overcome with emotion. She raised the ornate cup within her hands and spoke warmly.

"You have given me a great gift, in your son. He is true of heart and mind, a gentleman, and the one I have been searching for. In return I would like to give you a gift, something that is special to me. It represents who and what I am."

She gazed lovingly at the cup in her hands.

"It is a symbol of my love, a sealed chalice to show that I always look within for the answers that I need. I trust in how I feel and follow my heart in all things. I hope it will bring you great joy."

Lily thanked the Queen for such an offering, and they talked for many hours afterward, sharing their thoughts and musing on the power of love.

"I have always been governed by love," spoke Lily softly. "It is the one true emotion, and something my father taught me. He told me that every moment is an opportunity to give and receive love. A single moment can change your life forever."

The Queen smiled. "It is the moments that make up the rest of our lives, and we need to make the most of every single one." Then she paused, and together they raised the cup high. "To love, in all its many forms."

KING OF CUPS

THE WEDDING BETWEEN THE QUEEN and her Knight was the perfect celebration of love. While it was grand, it was also intimate and heartfelt. The ceremony was joyful, and there was much singing and laughter. The streets were lined with ribbons and flowers, and tables groaned with food. Children played, and even pretended to be the King and Queen, walking down the aisle. In the early evening the townsfolk collected in the square to applaud their new King and afterward there was more good-natured revelry. Bands played and people danced late into the evening.

Lily and her husband witnessed the entire event. It was the perfect day, and her only sadness was that her father could not be there to see the family they had created. He would have been proud and pleased that they had found such happiness, but her birth father, the artist, was there to share in the celebrations, and that filled her with joy.

Lily's son, the new King, sat upon his throne and took a moment to breathe, to let the events of the day sink in. From his position in the throne room he could see the sea and had the perfect view of the horizon. He watched the flow of the waves, and the pull of the tide. The ebb and flow became a pattern in his mind, and he matched his breathing to its gentle rhythm. The calmness washed over him, and he felt truly at peace. Every so often the surface of the ocean rippled, and a fish would leap from the water and catch his eye. It made him smile and reminded him that life was full of surprises; that one could never really know what the future holds.

He realized then how much he was drawn to the element of water, and how it had played a role in his life so far. When he'd first left home with no destination in mind, the river had called to him. He'd journeyed at its side, following the winding path that eventually led him to his true love. Not only that, but water also seemed integral to his mother too. It had kept her safe as a tiny babe when she'd been abandoned in the tall reeds. It had lured her father close and given them both something to love.

It made sense to the King, for emotions were like water; they could not be repressed. It was better to let them flow and to express feelings. Even so, there was balance to be found between the heart and head; he had learned this also. As King, he would be taking on a new role, one where he would need to be a compassionate leader, a reliable confidante to the Queen. He had vowed to be at her side, a loyal and supportive husband and guide, and this was his only mission in life.

As the clock struck midnight, and all around was calm, the King sat in silent contemplation. Content, and full of love, he gave thanks for the blessings in his life, for the love of his mother and father, and also the love that had brought them together. He gave thanks for the love of his people, and his beautiful Queen. And in that one moment, his cup overflowed with joy.

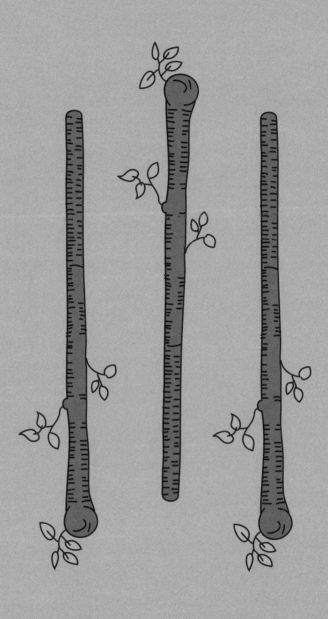

The Suit of Wands

ACE OF WANDS

ONCE UPON A TIME, THERE WAS AN IDEA, a kernel of a thought that had not yet been conceived. It had no shape or form, no color or movement, nothing that set it apart from any other idea. It simply was in existence somewhere in another realm—but where is anyone's guess, for really, how can we know the place that true inspiration comes from? And while you ponder that thought, consider how it arrives too. Is it a spark, a burst of light, or just a sense of knowing that fills your brain? Perhaps you see in colors, or you're blessed with a vision of how things could be. Indeed, ideas are as unique as the person who has them. But let's get back to this idea, the one in the story.

It sits all alone in a place that shall remain nameless, waiting to be born, to be plucked from the ether by someone who will make the most of it. It's hard to say how long it must wait, but time moves differently here than it does on Earth and the idea has nothing else to do. It would twiddle its thumbs, if it had some, but instead it learns to be hopeful, because as I'm sure you already know, ideas don't give up. They don't let boredom get the best of them. This idea was no exception and so it starts to imagine.

It imagines what it will be like to light someone up from the inside. To propel them forward, to be the fresh start, the new beginning, the plan that will change their life. And it gets carried away with itself, so much so that it begins to lengthen and stretch, to reach for the stars. The more it pictures what could be, the stronger and bigger it becomes until the idea is no longer formless, it stands tall and proud, an arrow with a target in mind. Excitement takes over and the arrow grows even more, like a new shoot bursting from the ground. It pushes on, and this time it becomes a wand, a powerful tool in the right hands and that's when you become aware of it. . . .

What you don't know is that this wand is special. It is strong, and ready to carry the flame of inspiration. It is the first of its kind, and like any Ace it heralds things to come. It is not just an idea, it is the potential to create anything you want. All you have to do is pick it up and let the magic happen . . . and that's exactly what the character in this story does. He takes the seed of an idea, and turns it into a story; his story.

TWO OF WANDS

THEMES

Future planning

Discovery

Decisions

Confidence

THE MAN, WHOSE NAME WAS WILLIAM, woke up with the spark of an idea in his head and that's how it started. Like a tiny flickering flame, he could feel it behind his eyes, lighting him up from the inside. For the first time in his young life, he felt truly inspired, bristling with an energy that seemed to take over his entire body. Up until that point, life had seemed rather dull. Opportunities had been scarce, and it was expected that he would follow on in the family business, carving and crafting tools, which would then be sold at market. While he had inherited the talent for working with wood, he had no particular passion for tool-making. He yearned for more, but up until that morning, he had no idea what "more" might be.

Now, with the germ of an idea nestled in his head, the young man was certain—it was time to make plans, to map out the future, and consider bigger and brighter aspirations. In his mind, he could see a vision of what he wanted to create. William had heard of other lands, magical places where tools held power, and each one was unique; where they were infused with an energy that could be used to manifest your heart's desire. He longed to know more, to combine the knowledge he already had with something new. The result would be a wand-like tool that could change the world and bring people together.

To do this, William would need to learn as much as he could, to look to others for their input and advice, and to plan out each stage of the process. While the crafting of the wand would come easy to him, there were other elements he would need help with. In his mind, he could see alliances forming. He imagined his enterprise going from strength to strength. No longer would this be a family business, it would take on a life of its own and spread throughout the known kingdom. His invention would be so popular that he would make a name for himself. He would have the world in his hands!

William sighed. Yes, he could see it clearly, and he could plan it in his mind, but now was the time for action, for taking that first tentative step toward success, and to do that he would have to leave behind all that he knew, to strive for a new goal. He knew in his heart it would be hard to move away from the fold and leave the security of the family business. It was not a decision to be made lightly, and yet, it was something he had to do.

The future was calling. The idea was growing. The promise of fulfillment was out there, and to find it he would have to take a leap of faith.

THREE OF WANDS

DRESSED IN A LONG, RED ROBE, and with three handcrafted staffs of the finest yew wood to demonstrate his skill, William stepped out into the world, leaving all that he knew behind him. He made his way to the edge of the sea. From here he could see everything. The vista was a blank canvas from which he could create something new. He could sense his excitement growing. Now was the time to broaden his horizons, to seek out different cultures and learn as much as he could, but to do this, he would need to venture farther afield.

To some, this would be a daunting task. William had never traveled anywhere before, but the idea propelled him forward. To bring his plan to fruition he needed to believe in himself and to commit to the process. And so it was that with a small amount of money that he'd managed to save and the offer of working to support his board, he secured a place on a ship. He knew not where it was going, only that it would be traveling to all four corners of the land, to kingdoms he had never even heard of. It would be an arduous journey, and not for the faint of heart, but William was prepared. In his heart he knew he had to do this to realize his dream.

The voyage was indeed treacherous, but it was also liberating; as William's self-belief grew, so did his knowledge. He learned how to navigate by the stars, how to control the ship, and work with the tides. He was an active part of the team, helping out on board and doing his bit. He made friends, confidantes, and also won admirers for his humility and willingness to learn. Most of all he discovered how to lead and inspire confidence in others.

He collected wisdom from around the world, in the form of stories and folklore. Every port had something to offer, and every type of people had something to share. Whether it was a skill, a trade, or a sprinkling of magic that he could use in his wands. William gratefully accepted it all because he knew it would help him reach his goal and create something truly unique.

The weeks and months soon passed, and before long William had reached the end of his journey, but he was much changed from the experience. No longer the young hopeful boy who had first stepped on deck, he was now a man with a vision and the passion and knowledge to accomplish it.

FOUR OF WANDS

WILLIAM HAD AT LAST MADE IT HOME. It had been more than a year, and although he had enjoyed his travels, he had missed his family. The sight of the shore and the beach that he recognized filled him with happiness. Laden with trinkets, treasures, and gifts, he made his way up the path, toward the road that led to his village. In the distance he could hear music playing, and voices raised in celebration.

It must be someone's birthday, or perhaps a wedding feast, he thought, as he neared the small square. It was tradition that the villagers would come together to mark special occasions; it helped to create harmony and build a sense of community. Slowly he mounted the hill and, as he reached the brow, he could clearly see the castle ahead and the square, which was decorated with an abundance of wreaths and vines. Whatever was happening, it was surely a grand affair.

"There he is!" a voice cried, and then more raised voices joined in. People were gathering in clusters, some of them jumping up and down and waving.

It took William a moment to realize that he was the center of attention. Then from out of the crowd came his parents; they were running toward him. His mother had her arms wide open, and his father was smiling broadly.

"Son, it is so good to have you home."

"How did you know that I would arrive this day?" asked an astonished William.

"We got word that the ship was nearing the coast yesterday, and hoped that you would be on board."

"You have returned to us," said his mother, patting him on his arm, "and look at you! You left us a boy and now you're a man."

William smiled. It felt good to be here, to be in the one place where he was truly loved. There was a sense of unity, a reassuring warmth that wrapped around him as he was welcomed by his family and friends.

"Let us celebrate your return!" said his father proudly, and everyone cheered.

They talked and laughed and shared tales long into the night. There was a great feast, and dancing too, and it seemed like the party would never end. It was a moment of recognition for William and a joyful reunion, but there was more work to come. For now he had all he needed to bring his masterplan to life. He just hoped that the rest of the village would see the potential and want to join in with his venture.

FIVE OF WANDS

THEMES

Disagreement

Conflict

Opposition

Chaos

FOR HIS WAND-MAKING ENTERPRISE TO WORK, William hoped to have a team of villagers on side—after all, he had big plans and he needed them to spread the word. With this in mind, he called together a meeting of some of the most learned minds. He would show them the wands he had already crafted and what they could do, and they would be awestruck by their power. He had gathered so much sacred knowledge that he now knew how to imbue the wood with a magical intent. He knew how to craft a wand that, with a flick of the hand and the correct words, could perform any spell. The wisdom from his travels meant that he could create wands that would heal, help, and also manifest great things. He had also come up with a way to make them unique, by borrowing symbols and patterns from the different lands he'd visited, which he used to decorate each one. William was so excited and couldn't wait to show the gathered group what he had created.

The villagers, for their part, were not expecting to see magical feats. They knew that William had big ideas but believed he would be showing them artifacts and ornaments inspired by his travels, and that this was what he wanted to sell.

"Wands?" one of them cried. "We do not support the dark arts!"

"But let me show you what they can do. They can be put to good use, you'll see."

"But they are wands! What are we supposed to do with them?"

"So many things," William urged. "Please give me a chance to explain what I have in mind."

The villagers weren't impressed and argued against the idea. William had not been expecting this conflict. He tried his hardest to negotiate, to get them to listen and understand, but his words fell on deaf ears. With everyone shouting to be heard, it was impossible to make any headway and William felt deflated.

"Please, just hold one, notice how it feels in your hands."

He tried one last time to generate some interest, but the villagers simply raised the wands in anger, and shook them at each other. The dispute swiftly escalated, and soon it felt like all of those gathered were caught in quarrels of their own making.

William shook his head in despair and watched as the wands that he had lovingly crafted were used as weapons, to thrash the air. This was not what he had intended, and it seemed that his dream was further away than ever.

SIX OF WANDS

THEMES

Success

Progress

Victory

Enthusiasm

Amidst the confusion, the idea that had blossomed in William's mind took hold once more and, as he drew a deep breath in, he felt the flame flicker. For a moment he lost sight of the chaos in front of him. It was as if the idea had taken over everything and he remembered why this was so important to him. He recalled what he had learned on his travels, and how that knowledge was key to his success. He remembered his mission, why the wands were so special, and that's how he knew what to do next.

Lifting a wand high into the air, he made a wish. He said the words in his head, and then out loud with as much passion as he could muster. He felt their power blend with the magic of the wand, and a tingle of excitement rushed through him. There was a small explosion, a fizzling sound in the air as the energy of his wish burst forth, and then nothing but stillness. For a moment William was unsure if it had worked, but then slowly and surely, the gathered group began to drop their weapons and hug each other. Words of friendship were once more uttered, and the atmosphere was calm. Faces were no longer twisted in anger; instead they were smiling and people were shaking hands and exchanging apologies.

"What just happened here?" asked one man, as he looked about him.

William grinned. "It was a healing of sorts. I simply made a wish, using this," and he offered his wand to the man, who tentatively studied it.

"This wand is capable of such goodness?" he asked.

"Yes," said William, "that's what I've been trying to tell you. The wands are not tools to be used in a negative way. They can bring hope and healing. They can help us do good things if we apply them in the right way."

The gathered group nodded slowly, as if the truth had finally dawned upon them.

"So this is what you want to create, to make the world a better place?"

"Yes, it is. It is my dream that we can make things better, using my wands to help us."

And so it was that the learned men listened intently to William's idea. They asked questions and they offered their support. They embraced his venture with enthusiasm, and the negativity that had clouded their thoughts was replaced by optimism and confidence.

The meeting was a victory, and with a team of supporters on board, William was assured of success. Feeling triumphant, he strode out on his white steed to meet the rest of the community and share the joy with them.

SEVEN OF WANDS

OVER THE NEXT FEW MONTHS, William and his team of trusty supporters worked hard to make the venture a success and, as word spread, he became inundated with new commissions. His wands were genuinely beautiful; not only to look at, but in the actions they could perform and the happiness they could bring. It was not surprising then that others tried to follow suit. Wood workers from the seven kingdoms decided to turn their hands to wand-making in a bid to share in the success, and while some had a natural talent, most struggled for they did not have the acquired knowledge or passion that William had.

Those who once admired him for his inventive ideas grew bitter. They desperately wanted to be as successful, and they couldn't understand why it was not happening. Instead they turned on him and did their best to slander his name and cause obstruction, spreading false rumors and challenging his true intentions. They put every kind of obstacle in his way.

William had suspected that this would happen. He knew that as his business grew it would cause envy and hate amongst those of a similar profession. While he was prepared for the difficulties that would come, he found himself constantly having to negotiate terms and appease buyers and sellers. He became ever more used to defending himself, and his good name.

In the end, William realized that he had to find a way through this period and find a way to keep everyone happy and protect his venture. But what could he do?

Looking at the wands within his grasp, he realized the answer had been there all along. He had made these tools and he knew how to work their magic. All he had to do was find a way to spread that healing magic, to overcome the obstacles he now faced. He would draw upon his self-belief and the power of communication to spread the love.

If he faced his oppressors with confidence and communicated his true purpose using the power of the wands to enhance the message, then surely he would win them around?

And so, working with his team, he made a set of seven magical wands, one for each kingdom that he needed to impress. He would personally visit each of his detractors and present them with this gift. He would use tact and diplomacy to sway their fears and get them on side. He would fight his corner, but he would do it with an open heart and mind, and hopefully they would respond in kind.

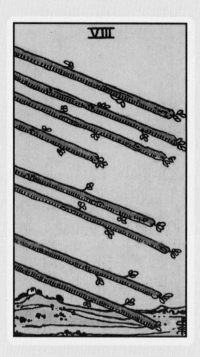

EIGHT OF WANDS

THE NEXT FEW MONTHS WERE A HIVE OF ACTIVITY, and William felt like he was caught in a whirlwind. He made a point of visiting all seven kingdoms personally, in a bid to charm his detractors and win favor. This meant much of his time was spent on the move, charting new territories and venturing into the heart of each kingdom. Again, it was a period of learning, a time to broaden his horizons and look to the future with optimism. Things were moving fast. He had set a catalyst in motion and he had to learn to go with the flow.

Communication was the key to everything, and William worked hard to build relations with all those he visited. He delivered his message with eloquence and spent time negotiating deals that ensured everybody would be happy with the outcome. He involved some of the wood workers who had taken against his initial plans and, by making them a part of the creative process, he was able to get them on side. He now had a team working for him in every kingdom and had become a man of great substance almost overnight. In return, the wood workers were fully dedicated, because they enjoyed their work and they cared about each wand they crafted.

William's intention was clear. He wanted the wands to work their magic, to bring people together, and create a sense of unity between all of the kingdoms. It seemed that his dream was being realized. Not only was he one of the most successful men in the known world, but he had also managed to build bridges and create harmony amongst the people. The energy that was once weighed down by jealousy was now light and full of hope, and everyone's spirits were lifted.

"You have done well, son," said William's father proudly. "You have achieved so much, but I wonder what is next upon your list?"

William sighed. "In all honesty, I do not know. I have not had the time or space to think about my next steps. Business is booming, and I am a success, but it has happened at such a speed. I feel like I have been swept off my feet."

"Then perhaps you need to slow down and enjoy the rewards of your hard work. We all need a moment of respite and time to recharge."

William agreed, but he had a strange feeling that this would not happen yet. His instincts told him there was something coming, something he had not foreseen, and this worried him deeply.

NINE OF WANDS

THEMES

Battle weary

Fatigue

Resilience

Last stand

As THE DAYS PASSED, WILLIAM GREW ever more weary. It was as if a dark cloud hovered above him and with every breath he could feel it pressing down, filling him with dread. And then one day, out of the blue, catastrophe hit in the form of a visitor from a distant land—a strange gray man wielding a wand that was not of William's making. There was something sinister in the way he moved. His entire presence was domineering, but more worrying than anything was the wand he held in his hands. The symbols etched into the wood were not sacred and imbued with good magic. They were dark, and deadly, and William knew instantly that this man had not come in peace.

"Wand maker, if that is what you call yourself," he called out. "I have traveled far to see the one who claims to make magical wands!"

"You are more than welcome, sir, I will happily show you my wares," replied William. If kindness and an open heart could soothe the situation, then he would try.

The gray man smiled, but it was without warmth.

"You mistake me. I do not want to see or delight in what you have created. You have exposed magic to the masses. You have taken arcane secrets, which should never have been shared, and let everyone see them. You are an abomination and I have come here to stop you. I challenge you to a fight."

William shivered. He had feared this was coming. Exhausted and weary from weeks of frenzied activity, he did not have the strength to face this opponent. He felt sure he would fail and all of his hard work would amount to nothing. And yet, what could he do? This was his last stand and he needed to rise to the challenge.

So it was that the stage was set for an almighty showdown. The gray man would not be dissuaded and William, despite the fatigue in his bones, needed to dig deep and find the resilience to face him.

One on one they stood facing each other with their wands primed. William's was imbued with love, and ready to protect all that he held dear, but the gray man had different ideas.

A terrible battle followed, and it brought great destruction. The gray man used his wand to send bolts of lightning in every direction. Buildings tumbled, roofs collapsed, and balls of fire rolled through the village. And still William stood firm. Despite the chaos, he held tight to his resolve. He had faith in his ability and the magic of his wand. He held the gray man off and when he could no longer shield himself, in a last attempt to salvage everything, he took a deep breath and pictured a very different scene. He saw what he wanted to create, his vision of peace—the gray man defeated, overwhelmed by the goodness in William's heart. Surrounded by a wall of wands, and himself suffering injury, he uttered this final spell and unleashed the power of love.

TEN OF WANDS

THE SPELL THAT WILLIAM CAST WITH HIS WAND called upon all of the sacred knowledge that he had gathered on his travels. As such it was universal, and the most powerful weapon that he could have unleashed. Love swept through the village and the kingdom in a wave of energy, knocking the gray man to the floor and overwhelming him. Within seconds all of the malice that lived within his heart was gone, replaced by an emptiness. The battle was over, and the gray man fled in confusion, for he couldn't recall why he was there or what he was doing—such was the might of William's magic.

Even so, the village and the neighboring town had suffered greatly during the attack. Homes were destroyed, walls and structures crumbling, and there was much to be done to put it right. William was distraught. He felt totally responsible for the devastation, even though he had not started the fight. He knew that it was down to him to make everything right, and so with the world upon his shoulders, he set to work.

Gathering up his tools and with a pile of wands in his arms, he trudged onward, mounting the hill that led to the town to begin rebuilding everything. It would be a long, slow process but William was prepared to work day and night. He was completely exhausted from the battle and his heart was heavy, but this was his duty.

The days that followed were arduous, and there were times when William thought he would not be able to continue. His entire body ached, his hands were calloused and bleeding, and his thoughts were as dark as the night. The villagers watched, and some even tried to help, but most stood in corners, talking in whispers. They blamed him for what had happened, and it would take some time for them to recover.

Luckily, William had plenty of that. He persevered, rising each day at dawn and working till dusk and, over the weeks, slowly but surely, the villagers' minds were swayed. They could see how much he cared, and how bad he felt. They also recognized the spirit and will that pushed him on. Soon an army of followers joined William in his efforts. They worked in teams, helping to labor and carry tools, to craft and rebuild walls, and to fix roofs.

By the time the fall came, the village and town were complete once more, and some even said they were better for the renovations. Some of the oldest structures were now more secure, and some of the newer buildings better in shape and style. This wasn't the only thing that had been repaired. William's reputation was once more salvaged, and the villagers and townsfolk acknowledged that they had all learned something from the experience.

PAGE of WANDS.

PAGE OF WANDS

THEMES

Optimism

Bright ideas

Energy

An enthusiastic
youngster

WINTER CAME AND WENT, and soon the lighter, brighter days were back again. Shoots began to burst through the soil to meet the sun, some bearing tiny buds ready to flower. Spring was taking hold, and it brought with it a feeling of optimism that could be felt in the early morning breeze. The coming of the season also heralded a new arrival to the village; a young, fresh-faced boy with a glint in his eye. He wore a feathered cap, a bright tunic, and he carried in his grip a large, leafy staff.

"I have come to learn how to make wands, to be an apprentice to the most famous wand maker in all of the kingdoms," he stated, to anyone who would stop and listen.

He was eager to pledge his loyalty and full of enthusiasm, but there was something else too; the way he held himself and the quality of his robes meant he was a young man of means. A quick learner and highly intelligent, it was obvious that this boy was accustomed to the very best of everything, a fact not lost on William.

"Are your parents happy that you have left home at such an early age to seek your fortune?"

"They will be happy when they see what I can do. They have a path in mind for me, but I have my own ideas."

This was clear to see, and William couldn't help but admire the boy's spirit. It reminded him of his own quest, and how he had left the comfort of the family home to make his dreams come true.

"I am willing to teach you all I know," he said, "but in return, you must send word to your family. Tell them where you are, and of your plans. Let them know that you are safe, and cared for, and that you will be staying with me over the summer."

The boy agreed, and so it was that over the months that followed, William had a new apprentice, a boy as bright and imaginative as he had once been. He worked hard, and studied everything that William did, copying, practicing, and perfecting his craft. He asked questions, he listened, and he learned, until there was nothing left to absorb. He had devoured every detail and was itching to make his mark.

"Master," he said, "I think it is time. I think that I am ready to come up with my own idea."

"And do you have something in mind?" asked William.

"I do," the boy smiled widely. "But first I must send for my family. I would like you to meet them."

KNIGHT OF WANDS

THEMES

Passion

Inspired action

A confident,
adventurous young
man

IT SEEMED TO WILLIAM THAT IN THAT MOMENT the boy grew into a man, and this was no subtle transformation. His apprentice seemed to swell with pride. It was as if the light that had been in his eyes was now a fire burning in his heart.

He sent word to his family that they should travel to the village and they would receive a warm welcome. On the day of their arrival, he was ready.

"I will ride out to meet them. It is what they will expect of me," he said. "But first I must change. I cannot greet them in my working clothes."

William nodded and watched as his apprentice disappeared into his room. Some time later he emerged, and the change that had been noted days earlier was even more evident. He moved with renewed confidence, holding his head high and with the grace of a ballerina, and yet he was strong, thick set in his armor. His yellow overgarment bore a salamander pattern, which William associated with the element of fire and one other thing—royalty. This was the color and design only worn by the King, and his sons. Taking a step back, William dropped to his knee.

"Your Majesty!"

The Knight of Wands, for that is what he was, raised a hand.

"Please, do not bow on my account. It is I who should bow to you. You have welcomed me into your home, taught me all you know, and helped me grow. I owe you a great debt, and I am sorry for any deception. All I wanted was the chance to follow my heart, to lead a normal life for a time, and learn a skill. I wanted to be accepted for who I am, rather than what I am. You have given me all of that and so much more."

The Knight stood rooted to the spot. His staff was more like a spear in his hand; fresh leaves were shooting from the wood, like ideas bursting forth from a fertile mind.

"I do not know what to say," William shook his head. "All of this time I have been hosting a Knight, teaching the King's son."

"And that is just as I wished. Your work is amazing and your intention true. I can see what you are trying to create, and I think it is time that you were honored for this."

The Knight turned then and mounted his horse. The chestnut steed whinnied and raised up its front legs.

"He is raring to go, and so must I!"

"Goodbye, fair Knight," cried William, but he was already gone, leaving behind a flurry of dust.

QUEEN OF WANDS

THE KNIGHT OF WANDS DID NOT HAVE TO TRAVEL FAR to encounter the royal entourage. They had set up camp overnight a few miles outside of the town. He wasn't sure what reception he would receive—after all, it was not normal practice for one of royal blood to do such a thing, but he hoped that his parents would see the change in him.

On arrival, the Queen was waiting for him, sitting on a golden throne that was ornately carved with lions to symbolize her strength, along with sunflowers synonymous with vitality. She was dressed in a sparkling robe to match her spirits.

"My boy," she said warmly, "or should I say young man, for you have grown in the time you've been away, like this sunflower that I hold in my hands."

The Knight bowed and smiled. "I have learned much. It has been an adventure."

"I can see that," said the Queen. "Tell me what you have learned. I want to know everything!"

And so the Knight regaled her with tales of his time as an apprentice. He told her about William and how he made the magical wands. He explained that they were imbued with happiness and love to unite people, to heal any rift, and the Queen was suitably impressed. Being a creative soul, her curiosity was piqued.

"I have always believed in following your dreams. Once you set your sights upon a goal, you should do everything in your power to make it happen."

William's story resonated with her deeply, and she felt the need to express her gratitude. The Queen was astute in her opinions and had always been a clever businesswoman.

She clapped her hands. "I must see these wands! I fancy that I would rather like one. I like to think of myself as a powerful woman."

Her son grinned. "I would agree with that."

"Well then, we must repay this man for all he has done, and all he hopes to do," she said triumphantly. "It seems we want the same thing—a kingdom united with joy—and I would like to do all I can to help William spread his message of harmony through the power of his wands."

The Knight bowed once more. "I will request an audience with the King and then take you both to meet him."

The Queen rose from her throne.

"Thank you my son, but before you go, one last thing." She paused. "Come here and give your mother a hug."

KING *of* WANDS

KING OF WANDS

IT DIDN'T TAKE THE ROYAL PARTY long to reach William's village and the workshop where he lived. There was a great commotion upon their arrival. The townsfolk and villagers gathered to see the regal procession in all its finery. They lined either side of the street, waving flags and banners, carrying baskets of fruit and flowers as gifts. A piper piped and a small choir collected to sing in honor of the King and Queen.

On alighting their carriage, the King set up his throne in the small square and waited for William to arrive. He looked every inch the visionary leader, with his plush red robe and cloak adorned with salamanders. His throne was equally impressive; larger salamanders were etched into the back of the seat to represent the element of fire, and the King's drive and leadership.

William was nervous. He knew what an honor it was to get a visit from the King, and he wanted to make a good impression. He polished his best wand and put on his finest garments, then made his way to the square.

The King was a fair and honest man, a leader who could take charge, and he always had a mission in mind. He wasted no time in thanking William for his efforts and for looking after his son. He was forthright and spoke with authority, and William listened intently and answered all his questions. Then, when it was called for, he withdrew his wand and cast a simple spell, and the air was filled with birdsong and butterflies. The royal entourage marveled at this magical feat, laughing and cheering.

The King rose and stepped down from his throne.

"I have never seen such a beautiful wand, nor have I ever known of a tool that could be used in such a positive way. Wands have in the past been used as weapons, but it is clear to see that your venture is rooted in peace."

William offered the wand to the King, for closer examination.

"William, would you do me the honor of kneeling before me?" The King smiled, then lightly he tapped him on both shoulders with the wand. "Arise, Sir William. I give you the greatest honor I can bestow, in recognition of what you have achieved so far."

The crowd roared in appreciation and William couldn't help but grin. All of those past trials and tribulations were now forgotten, all of his efforts worth it. He had fulfilled his wildest dreams and, in that moment, he was truly elated.

The King nodded. "In you, I see an accomplished man very much like myself. You know what you want and how to get it, and nothing can sway you from your cause. Let us work together to create a kingdom to be proud of."

The two men shook hands and the deal was sealed. From that moment on, William's venture went from strength to strength. The wands were universally accepted as symbols of harmony and accord, and the kingdom thrived.

CONCLUSION

The Tarot may seem enigmatic on the surface, and there's no doubt that magic can be found within the cards. After all, there's a reason they have survived, thrived, and evolved throughout the ages, going from parlor game for the upper classes to the divinatory tool of mystics and seers. The way the images resonate with our subconscious and shed light on the mind's hidden corners plays a part in their popularity, along with the sheer mystery and delight of "having" or "giving" a reading. There's a sense of the unexpected with the Tarot—who knows what secrets will be revealed, or what exciting events the future might hold? The more you learn about the cards, the more enthralled you become, and that's where the tales in this book can help. They offer a unique insight into each card's meaning and will help you connect spiritually and emotionally. Using stories to bring the deck to life helps to understand the Tarot's relevance today, and how you can harness the power of each card at a personal level.

Of course, there's more to it than simply reading and understanding the tales. You need to make it real for yourself by processing the themes within and applying them to your own situation. Asking questions such as: "How does this relate to my own life?" or "What part of this story rings true for me?" will help, along with addressing the most important question of all: "What is the core message within this tale?"

You can also connect to the power of each card by spending time in quiet reflection with it. Simply gaze at the image while running through the story in your mind, and see what develops. Allow yourself to daydream and get lost in the landscape of the Tarot.

Putting yourself within the story will bring new insights to light, whether you want to imagine that you're the main character or an onlooker. Either way, you'll gain a fresh perspective on the card and what it means to you. Retelling the tale in your own words helps to connect even deeper, so if you're feeling creative, try putting your own slant on things, or tell a different story. The wonderful thing about the Tarot is you can work with the cards in any way you please. You will develop your own relationship with the deck as you go along.

Most importantly, enjoy the journey, take it one step at a time as if you were turning the pages of a book, and seek pleasure from each story. There's no need to rush. Give your imagination free rein and see where the cards lead you. Wherever you end up, you'll be sure to have a Tarot adventure of epic proportions.

FURTHER READING

RESOURCES

Brigit Esselmont, *The Ultimate Guide to Tarot Card Meanings*
Mary K. Greer, *Tarot for Your Self*
Anthony Louis, *Tarot Beyond the Basics: Gain a Deeper Understanding of the Meanings Behind the Cards*
Sasha Fenton, *Fortune Telling by Tarot Cards*

ACKNOWLEDGMENTS

I would like to thank my lovely editor Chloe Murphy for all the effort and expertise she has put into this project, and for being the most uplifting and delightful lady to work with. I would also like to thank the rest of the team at Quarto, including the designer for helping to shape this special book.

I'd like to thank all of the Tarot readers who I have been lucky to learn from over the years and those who encouraged me on my own journey with the cards. It has been a lifelong passion of mine, and I, like anyone else who has succumbed to the magic of both the Major and Minor Arcana, will continue to find joy, inspiration, and wisdom from the tales behind the Tarot.

Index

First published in 2023 by Leaping Hare Press,
an imprint of The Quarto Group.
1 Triptych Place, London
SE1 9SH
United Kingdom
T (0)20 7700 6700
www.Quarto.com

A catalogue record for this book is available from the British Library.

ISBN 978-0-7112-8066-3
Ebook ISBN 978-0-7112-8067-0

10 9 8 7 6 5 4 3 2 1

Commissioning editor Chloe Murphy
Design by Ginny Zeal

Printed in China

Picture credits